MACBETH

Opera in Four Acts

Music by

Giuseppe Verdi

Libretto by
FRANCESCO MARIA PIAVE and ANDREA MAFFEI
(Based on Shakespeare's Play)

English Version by
WALTER DUCLOUX

Ed. 2755

G. SCHIRMER, Inc.

DISTRIBUTED BY
HAL•LEONARD® CORPORATION
7777 W. BLUEMOUND RD. P.O. BOX 13819 MILWAUKEE, WI 53213

Copyright © 1969 by G. Schirmer, Inc. (ASCAP) New York, NY
International Copyright Secured.   All Rights Reserved.
Warning: Unauthorized reproduction of this publication is
prohibited by Federal Law and subject to criminal prosecution.

Note

All rights of any kind with respect to this English translation and any part thereof, including but not limited to stage, radio, television performance, motion picture, mechanical, printing, and selling, are strictly reserved.

License to perform this opera in this translation in whole or in part must be secured in writing from the Publishers. Terms will be quoted upon request.

G. SCHIRMER, Inc.

MACBETH

The first product of Verdi's life-long enthusiasm for Shakespeare, *Macbeth* was written in the winter of 1846/47 when the composer was 33 years old. It still retains many of the earmarks of Verdi's intense and outspoken devotion to the cause of Italian independence. The ruthlessness of tyranny, the plight of its victims, the fiery call to arms by the liberator, most of these are found in every early Verdi opera, no matter what the setting or the period of the plot. Despite the fact that these subjects are treated as thinly disguised political propaganda, Verdi's passionate honesty and rhythmic and melodic power turn these moments into some of the most stirring episodes of his entire dramatic output.

As always, the fashioning of a play into an opera involves changes often painful to the admirer of the original. A number of scenes have to be sacrificed to make room for the proper domain of music: a slowly developing and enveloping mood that dispenses with the word, climactic moments of emotional explosion either in individual arias or ensembles during which the action is virtually suspended. Shakespeare's marvelous episode of the porter, pitting innocent ribaldry against horror, was left out. Several characters prominent in Shakespeare's play do not appear in the opera, including the "redeeming woman," Lady Macduff.

To compensate for this, Verdi's music brings to the drama its unique powers of atmosphere, character-delineation, and contrast. When told of Duncan's murder, the hastily summoned crowd bursts into a soul-shattering invocation of the wrath of God on the unknown assassin, in which both Macbeth and his wife must take part. In shivering whispers the guests react to Macbeth's vision of Banquo's ghost. The lugubrious English horn mimics the mournful cry of the hooting owl pursuing Lady Macbeth in her guilt-ridden sleep-walk.

As a contrast to the deepening gloom of the plot, Verdi endows the witches (embodied by three groups rather than individuals) and the murderers of Banquo with a kind of macabre humor. Totally unconcerned with the misery they cause, the witches see in the Thane of Glamis but a passing diversion on their never-ending pursuit of mischief, gloating at his torment as they feed him tantalizing tidbits of advance information. Banquo's killers — forerunners of Sparafucile — are calloused crooks to whom their grisly trade is a matter of sarcasm and a way of making a living.

First performed on March 14, 1847 in Florence, *Macbeth* reached Niblo's Garden in New York only three years later. In 1865, the composer revised and expanded the work for production in Paris. Although a relative failure at that time, this new version soon outdistanced the original and is generally performed today.

W.D.

CAST OF CHARACTERS

MACBETH } Generals in King Duncan's army . . . . } Baritone
BANQUO } .... } Bass
LADY MACBETH . . . . Soprano
LADY-IN-WAITING to Lady Macbeth . . . . Mezzo-Soprano
MACDUFF, Thane of Fife . . . . Tenor
MALCOLM, Duncan's son . . . . Tenor
A PHYSICIAN . . . . Bass
A SERVANT of Macbeth . . . . Bass
A CUTTHROAT . . . . Bass
A HERALD . . . . Bass
HECATE, the Goddess of the Night

King Duncan, Fleance (son of Banquo), Witches, Messengers of the King, Scottish Nobles and Refugees, Cutthroats, English Soldiers, Bards, Spirits of the Air, Apparitions.

The action takes place in Scotland, mainly in and around Macbeth's castle.
The 4th Act begins near the border between Scotland and England.

SYNOPSIS OF SCENES

			Page
Act I	Scene 1	A forest	4
	Scene 2	A hall in Macbeth's castle	38
Act II	Scene 1	A room in the castle	112
	Scene 2	A park near Macbeth's castle	121
	Scene 3	The banquet hall	134
Act III	A dark cave	192
Act IV	Scene 1	The Scottish-English border	258
	Scene 2	A hall in Macbeth's castle	278
	Scene 3	Another hall in the castle	291
	Scene 4	A vast plain	301

MACBETH

**English version by
Walter Ducloux**

Giuseppe Verdi

ACT I

Prelude

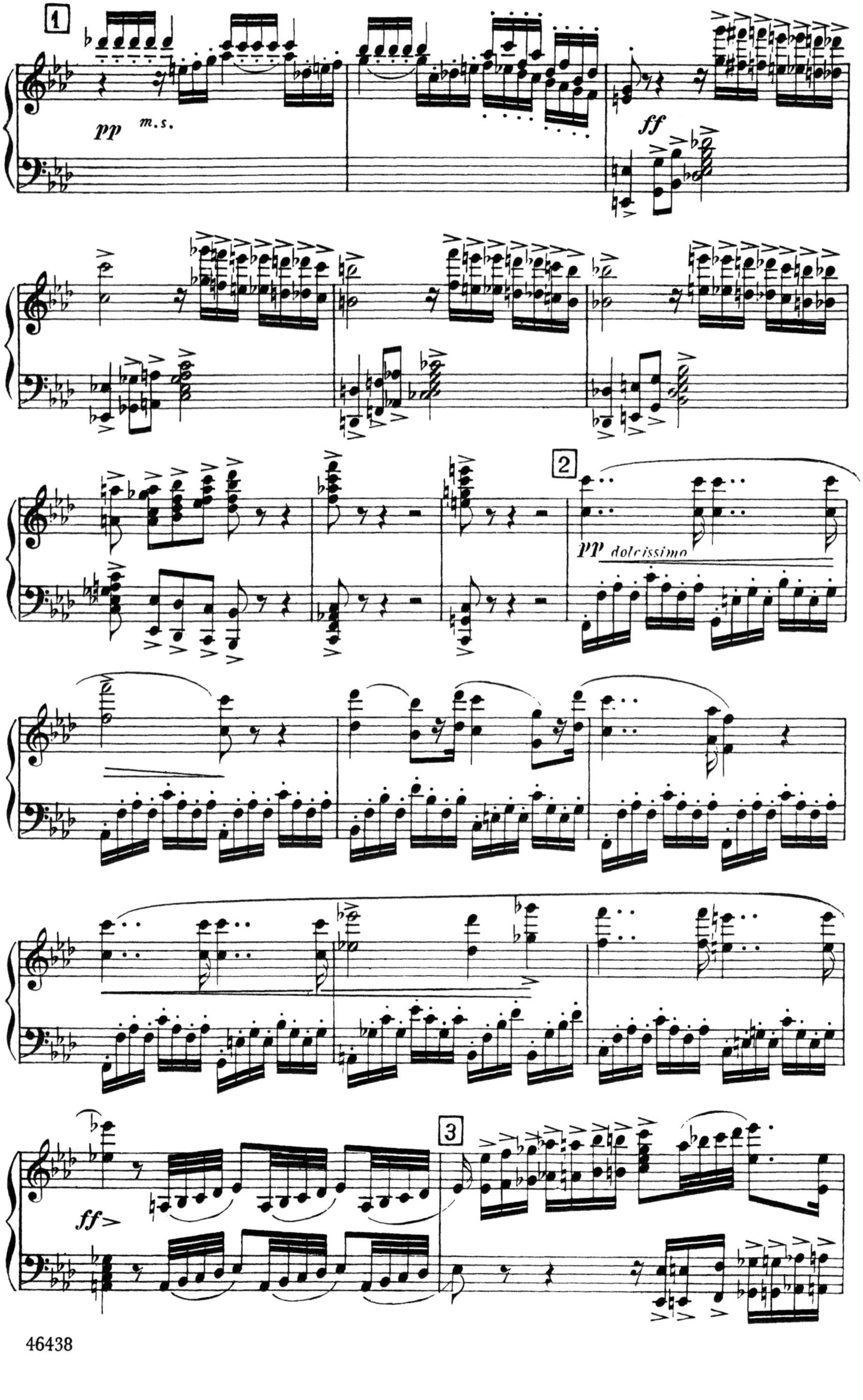
1
pp
m.s.
ff
2
pp dolcissimo
ff
3

3

Scene 1
A Forest

(Three groups of witches appear, one after the other, amid thunder and lightning.)

(Thunder and lightning; the first group of witches appears.)

(Thunder and lightning; the second group of witches appears.)

(Thunder and lightning; the third group of witches appears.)

6

S.i I.i
ma lo spo - - so, ma lo spo_so che sal_pò col suo le - - -
But her lov - - - er is a sail-or on the sea. He'll dis-cov - - -
tr
S.i I.i
gno, còl sùo legno affo_ghe_rò.
er just how mean a witch can be!
ff
Sop. I.i
cresc.
Per le sec_che lo trar_
Drown the vil-lain like a
Sop. 2.i
cresc.
I ma_rosi io le_ve_rò...
Wind and storm be fan-cy- free!
Sop. 3.i
p cresc.
Un ro_va_io ti da_rò...
Tid-al wave be sent by me,
pp
f
rò, per le secche lo trar_rò, per le secche lo trar_rò, per le secche lo trar_
flea, drown the vil-lain like a flea, drown the vil-lain like a flea, drown the vil-lain like a
i ma_rosi io le_ve_rò, i ma_rosi io le_ve_rò, i ma_rosi io le_ve_
Wind and storm be fan-cy- - free, wind and storm be fan-cy- - free, wind and storm be fan-cy-
un ro_va_io ti da_rò, un ro_va_io ti da_rò, un ro_va_io ti da_
tid-al wave be sent by me, tid-al wave be sent by me, tid-al wave be sent by
pp staccate assai
pp
ff
pp e staccate assai

4
rò, sì, per le sec-che lo trar-rò, per le secche lo trar-
flea! Ah, drown him, drown him like a flea! Drown the vil-lain like a
rò, ah, sì, i ma-ro-si le-ve-rò, i ma-ro-si le-ve-
free! Ah, storm and wind be fan-cy-free, storm and wind be fan-cy-
rò, ah, sì, un ro-va-io ti da-rò, un ro-va-io ti da-
me! A tid-al wave be sent by me, tid-al wave be sent by
rò, per le secche lo trar-rò, sì, per le sec-che lo trar-
flea, drown the vil-lain like a flea! Ah drown him, drown him like a
rò, i ma-ro-si le-ve-rò, ah, sì, i ma-ro-si le-ve-
free! Be for-ev-er fan-cy-free! Ah, storm and wind be fan-cy-
rò, un ro-va-io ti da-rò, ah, sì, un ro-va-io ti da-
me, Be a wit-ch's gift from me! A tid-al wave be sent by
rò, per le secche lo trar-rò, per le secche lo trar-rò, per le secche lo trar-
flea, drown the vil-lain like a flea, drown the vil-lain like a flea, drown the vil-lain like a
rò, i ma-ro-si le-ve-rò, i ma-ro-si le-ve-rò, i ma-ro-si le-ve-
free, storm and wind be fan-cy-free! Be for-ev-er fan-cy-free! Howl-ing wind up-on the
rò, un ro-va-io ti da-ro, un ro-va-io ti da-rò,
me! Tid-al wave be sent by me, Be a wit-ch's gift from me!

rò, io lo trar-rò, per le secche lo trar-rò, sì, lo trar-rò, sì, lo trar-rò.
flea there in the sea! Drown the vil-lain like a flea there in the sea! Out in the sea!

rò, io le-ve-rò, i maro-si le-ve-rò, sì, le-ve-rò, sì, le-ve-rò.
sea be fan-cy-free! Howling wind up-on the sea be fan-cy-free! For-ev-er free!

io ti da-rò, io ti da-rò, io ti da-rò.
A gift from me! A tid-al wave be sent by me.

(Snaredrum offstage.)

Un tam-bu - ro! Che sa-rà?
Who is near us? Hold your breath!

Un tam-bu - ro! Che sa-rà?
Who is near us? Hold your breath!

Un tam-bu - ro! Che sa-rà?
Who is near us? Hold your breath!

46438

ALL°. BRILLANTE 𝅗𝅥 = 144
Vien Mac - bet - to. Ec - co - lo qua.
Hail the he - ro! Here comes Mac - beth!
ff
p
ALL°. BRILLANTE 𝅗𝅥 = 144
5
p
stacc.
(All in one group, the witches begin a whirling dance.)
tr
p
Le so - rel - le va - ga - bon - de van per l'a - ria, van sul -
Hur - ry on! With bolt and thun - der let us tear the air a -
legg.

l'on_de, sanno un cir_co_lo intrec_cia_re che com_prende e terra e
sun-der! Fly a-way to plague and plun-der, roam-ing wide and roam-ing
l'on_de, sanno un cir_co_lo intrec_cia_re che com_prende e terra e
sun-der! Fly a-way to plague and plun-der, roam-ing wide and roam-ing
l'on_de, sanno un cir_co_lo intrec_cia_re che com_prende e terra e
sun-der! Fly a-way to plague and plun-der. roam-ing wide and roam-ing
ff
mar, sanno un cir_col in_trec_cia_re che com_prende e terra e
far! Blight and blun-der, plague and plun-der. Roam-ing wide and roam-ing
ff
mar, sanno un cir_col in_trec_cia_re che com_prende e terra e
far! Blight and blun-der, plague and plun-der. Roam-ing wide and roam-ing
ff
mar, sanno un cir_col in_trec_cia_re che com_prende e terra e
far! Blight and blun-der, plague and plun-der. Roam-ing wide and roam-ing
8
ff
mar, sanno un cir_col in_trec_cia_re che com_prende e terra e
far! See us. Sa-tan, plague and plun-der! Call on us and there we
mar, sanno un cir_col in_trec_cia_re che com_prende e terra e
far! See us, Sa-tan, plague and plun-der! Call on us and there we
mar, sanno un cir_col in_trec_cia_re che com_prende e terra e
far! See us, Sa-tan, plague and plun-der! Call on us and there we
8

13

(The witches are whirling around.)

mar. Le so-rel-le va-ga-bonde van per l'a-ria, van sul
are! Hur-ry on! With bolt and thun-der let us tear the air a-

mar. Le so-rel-le va-ga-bonde van per l'a-ria, van sul
are! Hur-ry on! With bolt and thun-der let us tear the air a-

mar. Le so-rel-le va-ga-bonde van per l'a-ria, van sul
are! Hur-ry on! With bolt and thun-der let us tear the air a-

l'onde, sanno un cir-co-lo intrec-cia-re che com-prende e terra e
sun-der! Fly a-way to plague and plun-der, roam-ing wide and roam-ing

l'onde, sanno un cir-co-lo intrec-cia-re che com-prende e terra e
sun-der! Fly a-way to plague and plun-der, roam-ing wide and roam-ing

l'onde, sanno un cir-co-lo intrec-cia-re che com-prende e terra e
sun-der! Fly a-way to plague and plun-der, roam-ing wide and roam-ing

mar, che com-prende e terra e mar, che com-prende e terra e
far, one, two, three and there we are! One, two, three and there we

mar, che com-prende e terra e mar, che com-prende e terra e
far, one, two, three and there we are! One, two, three and there we

mar, che com-prende e terra e mar, che com-prende e terra e
far, one, two, three and there we are! One, two, three and there we

15

16

(Macbeth and Banquo appear.)
ALLEGRO MAESTOSO ♩ = 104

MACBETH

REC.^{tivo}

Giorno non vi di mai_ sì fiero e bello!
Ah, what a day of fortune, of gore and glo-ry!

(noticing the witches)
Oh, chi saran co_stor?
Ah!___What are these?

BANCO

Nè tanto glorioso!
A day to re-mem-ber!

Chi siete vo_i? Di questo mondo, o d'altra re_gione? Dirvi donne vor_re_i, ma lo mi
Tell us: Who are you? Could you be hu-man, or should I call you demons? I could greet you as wom-en, and yet, those

B
MAC.
vieta quella sor-di-da barba. Or via par-la-te!
whisk-ers, they be-lie your ap-pear-ance. Speak out: Who are you?
AND.te SOST.to ♩=84
pp
CORO DI STREGHE
Sop. I.i
Sop. 2.i
Sop. 3.i (prophetically)
Salve, o Mac-bet-to, di Glamis si- - - re!
All hail, Mac-beth, o proud thane of Gla- - - mis!
Salve, o Mac-bet-to,
All hail, Mac-beth, o
di Cau-dor si- - - re!
proud thane of Caw- - - dor!
Salve, o Mac-bet-to, di Scozia re!
All hail, Mac-beth, who soon shall be King.
(Macbeth trembles.)
pp
f
ff
8
BANCO
(aside to Macbeth)
Tremar vi fanno così lie-ti au-guri?
Why are you trem-bling when fore-told good for-tune?
p
pp
ppp
morendo

(to the witches)
B
Fa_vellate a me pur, se non v'è scu_ro, cre_a_tu_re fan_tastiche, il fu_turo.
I command you, mys-te-rious, ghost-ly crea-tures, To re-veal me my fu-ture's hid-den fea-tures!
p
CORO DI STREGHE
Sop. I.
Salve!
Hail!
Sop. 2.
Salve!
Hail!
Non quanto lui, ma più di lui fe_li - ce!
Al-though less hap-py, you will yet be hap - pier!
Sop. 3.
Lo stesso tempo
Salve!
Hail!
Men sa_rai di Mac_bet_to e pur maggio - - re!
Though less great than Mac-beth, you will be great - - er!
9
Lo stesso tempo
pp
pp
Non re, ma di mo_narchi ge_ni_to - re!
Not King yourself, of kings you'll be a fa - ther!

ALLEGRO 𝅗𝅥 = 104
(All the witches disappear)
Mac_betto e Ban_co vi_va_no! Banco e Macbet_to vi - va_no!
Hail to Mac-beth, to Ban-quo, hail! Hail to Mac-beth, to Ban - quo, hail!
Mac_betto e Ban_co vi_va_no! Banco e Macbet_to vi - va_no!
Hail to Mac-beth, to Ban-quo, hail! Hail to Mac-beth, to Ban - quo, hail!
Mac_betto e Ban_co vi_va_no! Banco e Macbet_to vi - va_no!
Hail to Mac-beth, to Ban-quo, hail! Hail to Mac-beth, to Ban - quo, hail!
ALLEGRO 𝅗𝅥 = 104
10
mf
MAC.
REC.vo
Va_nir!
They're gone!
pp
(thoughtfully)
M
Saranno i figli tuoi so_vrani!_
They said your children would be kings! _
LARGO
sotto voce
morendo
Ac_centi ar_ca - ni!
Fate-ful fore-bod - ing!
BANCO
E tu re pria di loro. Ac_centi ar_ca - ni!
You, as king, would pre-cede them! Fate-ful fore-bod - ing!
LARGO
pp
(Enter the King's Messengers)
ALL.o RISOLUTO
𝅗𝅥 = 126
ff
ff

20

MESSAGGERI
Pro Macbetto, il tuo signore sir t'elesse
Hail, Macbeth! Your King and Sov'reign has proclaimed you

di Cau_dore.
thane of Cawdor.

MAC.
Ma quel si_re ancor vi regge!
The thane you mention still rules his people.

MES. No! percosso dalla legge sotto il ceppo egli spi_rò.
No! A trai_tor, on the rack he felt the justice of the law.

BANCO (aside, with a shudder)
Ah! Ah! l'in_fer_no il ver, il ver par_
Ah! (Hell-ish de_mons! So soon your words come

iò!
(true!)

AND.te ASSAI SOST.to ♩=50.

MAC. *(aside, softly, as if terrified)*

Due va_ti_ci_ni compiuti or sono... mi si pro_
If twice did hap - pen what they fore-told me, Pro-phet-ic

met_te dal ter_zo un trono... Ma perchè sen_to riz_zarsi il
vi_sions of a throne now hold me... Why am I dream-ing of blood and

(breaking out) *(darkly)* *(with full voice)*

crine? Pensier di san_gue, d'on_de_sei_nato? Al_la co_
hor-ror, My con-science teem-ing with_fear_and_ sor-row? If Fate should

M
ro - na che m'offre il fa - to la man ra -
will me a roy - al man - tle, Why, chance may
cresc.
pa - ce non alzerò non al - ze - rò.
crown me with-out my stir, with-out my stir.
BANCO
(aside, softly and haltingly)
Oh, come s'empie costui d'or -
His whole de-mea-nor be-trays am -
pp stacc.
go - glio nella speran - za d'un re - gio - so - glio!
bi - tion, Be-trays be-lief in what they said to be his mis - sion!
Due va - ti - cini compiu - ti or
Twice did it hap-pen, what here the demons
B
pp
12

23

sono....
told me...

Ma spesso l'empio spirto d'a_ver_no parla, e c'ingan_na, vera_ci
And yet, the de-mons, the fiends of dark-ness, With hon-est tri-fles of-ten may al-lay sus-

mi si promette dal ter_zo un trono!   mi si promet __ te, mi si pro
Why should not vi-sions of throne and glo-ry hold me?   En-chant-ing vi - sions of throne and

det _ ti,   e ne abbando __ na poi maledet _ ti
pi - cion,   On-ly to lead us in-to per-di - tion.

met __ te dal ter _ zo, dal ter _ zo un trono!   Ah!__
glo __ ry, Why should they, why should they not hold me? Ah!

su quell'abis _ so _ che _ ci _ sca_vò, e ne abbandona maledetti....
Far off the path on which we blindly thought we were! They lead us on in-to per-di-tion..

46438

(with full voice)
M
Ma perchè sento rizzar - si il cri - ne?
Why am I dream-ing of blood and hor - ror?
B
Ma spesso l'em - pio spir - to d'a -
And yet, the de - mons, the fiends of
p
con slancio
stent.
M
Pen - sier di sangue, d'onde sei na - to?
Why is my mind, why my heart filled with sor - row?
B
ver - no parla, e c'ingan - na, vera - - ci
dark - ness, With hon-est tri-fles of-ten may al-lay sus -
M
Al - la co - ro - na che m'offre il fa - to la man ra -
If Fate should will me a roy - al man - tle, Why, chance may
B
det - ti, e ne ab - ban - do - na poi ma - ledet - - - - -
pi - cion. At last to lead us in - to per - di - - - - -

25

26

Chorus of Witches

S'allon_ta_na_ro_no! ... N'ac_coz_ze_re_____ mo quando di ful_mi_ni lo scro_scio u_

Be gone! A-way! Be gone! ... We'll meet a-gain_____ In thun-der and light-ning and fi_ery

29

ten - - - - - da le sorti a com - pie - re nel - la tre -
gain, _____ Fore-bod-ing and fright' - ning, to sit in

genda. Mac - bet - to rie - de - re
ju - ry. Send - ing a rake _____ to dam -

ve - drem co - là, e il no - stro o - ra - co - lo
na - tion and death, Tend - ing the wake for the

ve - drem co - là, e il no - stro o - ra - co - lo
na - tion and death, Tend - ing the wake for the

ve - drem co - là, e il no - stro o - ra - co - lo
na - tion and death, Tend - ing the wake for the

f caratteristico

gli par - le - rà. Mac - bet - to rie - de - re
might - y Mac - beth: He will re - turn for the

gli par - le - rà. Mac - bet - to rie - de - re
might - y Mac - beth: He will re - turn for the

gli par - le - rà. Mac - bet - to rie - de - re
might - y Mac - beth: He will re - turn for the

46438

ve - drem co - là, e il no-stro o - ra - co-lo
se - crets we keep, Burn - ing to learn what will

gli par - le - rà. Fug-giam, fuggiam, fug-giam, fuggiam! s'at-
slaugh - ter his sleep. A - way, un - til we meet a - gain in

ten - da le sor - ti a com - pie - re nel - la tre -
thun-der, light-ning, or in rain! In storm and night the witch-es sit in

ten - da le sor - ti a com - pie - re nel - la tre -
thun-der, light-ning, or in rain! In storm and night the witch-es sit in

ten - da le sor - ti a com - pie - re nel - la tre -
thun-der, light-ning, or in rain! In storm and night the witch-es sit in

genda. Fug-giam, fug-giam, fuggiam, fug-giam, sì fuggiam, fug-
ju-ry. Be gone! A - way! Let's flee un - til we will meet a -

genda. Fug-giam, fug-giam, fuggiam, fug-giam, sì fuggiam, fug-
ju-ry. Be gone! A - way! Let's flee un - til we will meet a -

genda. Fug-giam, fug-giam, fuggiam, fug-giam, sì fuggiam, fug-
ju-ry. Be gone! A - way! Let's flee un - til we will meet a -

46438

giam, fuggiam, fug-giam, fuggiam, fug-giam, sì, fuggiam, fug-
gain! Be gone! A - way! Let's flee un - til we will meet a -

giam! Macbet - to rie - de - re ve - drem, vedrem co - là, vedrem co -
gain! The ser - vants we of doom and death Will now for - ev - er haunt Mac-

là, _____ ed il nostro, il nostro o _ ra _ co _ lo gli par _ le _
beth. _____ We will tor - ment him re - lent - less - ly un - til his fi - nal

là, _____ ed il nostro, il nostro o _ ra _ co _ lo gli par _ le _
beth. _____ We will tor - ment him re - lent - less - ly un - til his fi - nal

là, _____ ed il nostro, il nostro o _ ra _ co _ lo gli par _ le _
beth. _____ We will tor - ment him re - lent - less - ly un - til his fi - nal

rà, Macbet _ to rie _ de _ re ve _ drem, vedrem co _ là, vedrem co _
breath! The ser - vants we of doom and death Will now for - ev - er haunt Mac-

rà, Macbet _ to rie _ de _ re ve _ drem, vedrem co _ là, vedrem co _
breath! The ser - vants we of doom and death Will now for - ev - er haunt Mac-

rà, Macbet _ to rie _ de _ re ve _ drem, vedrem co _ là, vedrem co _
breath! The ser - vants we of doom and death Will now for - ev - er haunt Mac-

46438

là, _____ ed il nostro, il nostro o_ra_co_lo gli par_le_
beth. _____ We will tor-ment him re-lent-less-ly un-til his fi-nal

rà. Fug_giam, fug_giam, fuggiam, fug_giam, fuggiam, fug_giam, fug_
breath! Fly on, fly on! You witch-es, fly a-way, be gone! Fly

37

Scene 2

ALLEGRO ♩ = 92 A Hall in Macbeth's Castle.

(Lady Macbeth enters, reading a letter.)

LADY

Nel dì della vittoria io le incontrai... stupito io n'era per le udite cose; quando i nunzi del re mi
They met me on the day of my victory. While I stood rapt in the wonder of it came messengers from the king

salutaro sir di Caudore; vaticinio uscito dalle veggenti stesse che predissero un serto al capo mio.
who hailed me "Thane of Cawdor"; by which title these weird sisters had called me earlier, hinting later that I should

Racchiudi in cor questo segreto. Addio.
be king. Keep this in your heart, and farewell!

Am bizioso spirto tu sei, Macbet to... alla grandezza a
Proud is your heart and noble, filled with am-bi-tion. Yet on your path to

neli... ma sarai tu mal_vagio?
power, dare you re-sort to e-vil?

40

LADY

Pien di mi-sfat - - - ti è il cal - le del - la po-ten-za,
Haunt-ed by crime lies the road to great-ness and glo-ry.

e mal per lui che il piede dubitoso vi pone, e retro-ce - - - - -
Woe un-to him who, fear-ful, af-ter trying to climb it, Will then sur-ren - - - - -

- - - de!
- - - der!

41

42

43

L
pp
gnar. Che tar_di?Accetta il do _ no, ascendivi a re _ gnar. Che tar_di?Accetta il
star! Why wa-ver in the face of des-ti-ny? The die is cast, the goal not far. Behold, Macbeth, the prize I
ppp
do _ no, a_scen _ _ di _ vi a re _ gnar. Che tar _ _ _ di? Che tar _ _
ten _ der Go on _ _ ward to your might-y star! Why wa _ _ _ ver? Why wa _ _
f
ppp
di? Ah! ascendivi a re_gnar.
ver? Ah! On to your might-y star!
ppp
21 ALLEGRO 𝅗𝅥 = 96
p

45

(A servant enters.)

SERVO: Al cader della sera il re qui giunge.
The King of Scotland will visit here this evening.

LADY: Che di'?
To-night?

SERVO: Macbetto è seco?
Macbeth is with him?

Ei l'accompagna. La nuova, o donna, è certa.
Yes, he'll escort him, a liegeman proud and loyal.

LADY. *a piacere*
Trovi accoglienza quale un re si
He'll find a welcome most triumphant and

(The servant exits.)
L
mer - ta.
roy - al.
22
f
ff
a piacere
Dun - ca - no sa - rà qui?
King Dun-can here to - night?
col canto
pp
tutta forza
Qui?
Here?
Qui la not -
Here this eve -
te?
ning?
ff

47

LADY **ALL⁰. MAESTOSO** ♩=104 *a poco a poco cresc.*

Or tut - ti sor - ge - te, mi -
You fu - - ries of Sa - tan, as -

ALL⁰. MAESTOSO ♩=104

pp

ff

ni - stri in - fer - na - li, che al san - gue in - co -
sist me in my du - - ty! Un - sex me, hell - ish

ra - te, spin - ge - te i mor - ta - - li, che al
de - - mons, and fill my veins with gall! Drown what's

46438

sangue incora-te i mor-ta-
hu - man in poi - son and gall, ah!

li!   Tu, not - te, ne av - vol - gi di
       May night shroud in dark - ness the

te - nebra im - mo - ta; qual pet - to per-
mon - strous hour of hor - ror, Lest sight should warp the

co - ta non veg - ga il pu - gna - le, qual
dag - ger. in cruel light A kill-er stag - ger be-

L
pet - to per - co - ta non veg - ga, non veg - ga il pu -
fore the deed is done, ah, Be - fore the blow can
8
gnal, qual pet - to per - co - ta non veg - - - - - -
fall! In dark - ness be - shroud - ed the blow that soon will fall.
pp
- ga, no, no, non veg - - - - - - - - - - - - ga il pu -
ah, the blow, ah! that soon will
f
gnal.
fall!
24
8
ff
4 3 2 1 4 3 2 1 4 3 2 1 4 3 2 1
8

50

LADY

1.° TEMPO ♩ = 104 *a poco a poco cresc.*

Or tut—ti sor—ge—te, mi—
You fu—ries of Sa—tan, as—

ni—stri infer—na—li che al san—gue in co—
sist—me in my du—ty! Un—sex me, hell—ish

ra—te, spin—ge—te i mor—ta—li, che al
de—mons, and fill my veins with gall! Drown what's

46438

san - gue incora - te i mor - ta - - - - - - li! Tu notte ne av - vol - gi di te - nebra im - mo - ta; qual pet - - to per - co - ta non veg - ga il pu - gna - le, qual

hu - man in poi - son and gall, ah! May night shroud in dark - - ness the mon - strous hour of hor - ror, Lest sight should warp the dag - ger, in cru - el light A kill - er stag - ger be -

52

53

(Macbeth enters.)
ALLEGRO
MACBETH
LADY
MAC.
REC.vo
Oh donna mi-a! Caudo - re!
My no-ble la-dy! O Caw-dor!
Fra poco il re ve-
The King is on his
M
LADY
MAC.
LADY
dra-i... E parti - rà? Domani. Mai non ci rechi il so - le un tal do -
way here. When will he leave? To-mor-row. Ah, may the sun not shine on such a
L
MAC.
LADY
MAC.
ma-ni. Che parli? E non in - ten - di? In - ten-do, in - ten - -
mor-row! What are you say ing? Why must you ask me? I heard you! I heard
27
M
LADY
MAC.
LADY
do! Or bene? E se fallisse il colpo? Non falli - rà... se tu non tremi.
you! A-greed then? What if the plan mis-car-ries? It will suc-ceed, un-less you weak-en!

Il re!
The King!

Lieto or lo vieni, lieto or lo vie-
Come, let us greet him! Be of good cheer, ah!

ni ad incontrar con me.
Leave all the rest to me!

(Country-music, gradually nearing, announces the arrival of King Duncan. He crosses the stage, escorted by Banquo, Macduff, Malcolm, Macbeth, Lady Macbeth and his retinue.)

56

mf (The music becomes more and more distant.)

58

(Macbeth alone, to a servant)
parlante
MACBETH
Sappia la sposa mi_a, che pronta ap_pena la mia tazza not_
Go, tell your no-ble mis-tress to make quite cer-tain that, when my drink is
p
RECITATIVO
(The servant exits.)
M
turna, vo'che un toc_co di squilla a me lo avvi_si.
read-y, she strike up-on a bell to serve me no-tice!
ADAGIO
ppp
(The ensuing duet must be projected in a hushed and dark voice, except for some outbursts clearly marked "With full voice".)
f
ALLEGRO ♩= 126
ff
MACBETH
ALL°.
Mi si affaccia un pu_gnal?! L'elsa a me
'Tis a dag - ger I see, hilt turned up-

volta? Se larva non sei tu, ch'io ti bran-
on me! Unless you are a vision, here, let me

di_sca.... Mi sfuggi? Eppur ti veggio!
wield you! You flee me... yet I still see you!

LARGO ♩ = 50
A me pre_cor ri sul confu_ _so cam_
You lead me on a_long the path _ _way to

cupo e più piano che sia possibile

min che nel _ _ la men _ te di seguir di se_
crime, A_long the course my wan_ton con _ _science has

gnava! Orrenda im-ma — — — — — go!
cho-sen. Un-ho-ly phan — — — — tom!

Solco san-guigno la tua lama ir-ri-ga! Ma nulla esiste an-
Dark off your blade the drops of blood fall like weep-ing. And yet, in truth there's

cora... il sol cru-ento mio pensier le dà forma, e come vera mi presenta allo
noth-ing. 'Tis but a fig-ment of a mind in con-fu-sion that hangs before me, de-ceiv-ing my

sguardo una chi — me — ra.
eyes, a weird il-lu — sion!

misterioso

Sulla metà del mondo or morta è la na-
Death-like, on half the world has dark-ness spread her

tura: or l'assassino come fantasma per l'ombre si
mantle. Silent, the murd'rer stalks through the night on his way to dam-

striscia: or consuman le streghe i lor mi-
nation. Hour of gloom when the witches perform their

ALLEGRO ♩=100

steri. Immobil terra! a' passi miei sta muta!
mischief! Earth, firmly rooted, oh let my steps be muted!

Grave ppp

63

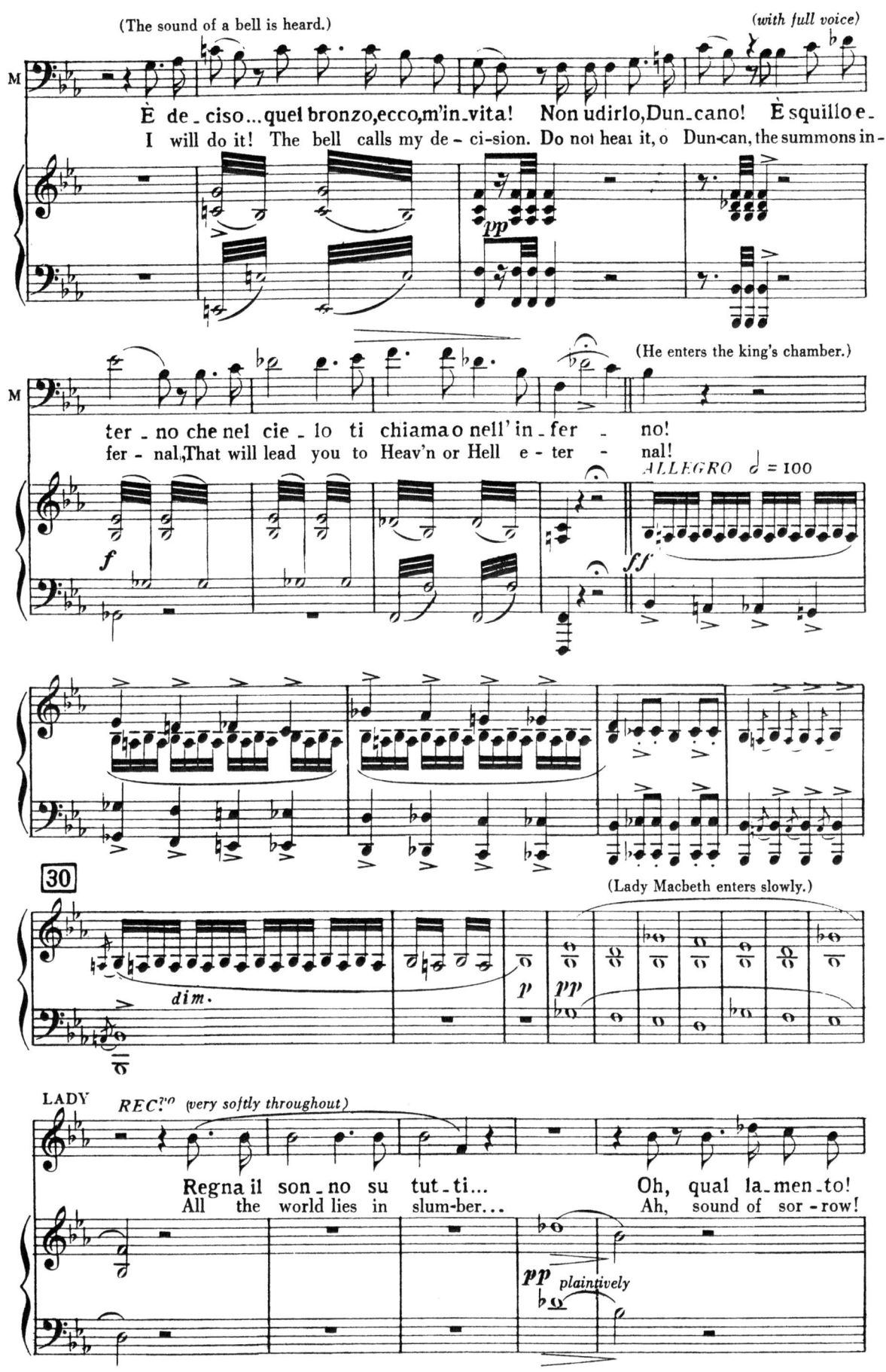

(The sound of a bell is heard.) (with full voice)

È deciso... quel bronzo, ecco, m'invita! Non udirlo, Duncano! È squillo e-
I will do it! The bell calls my decision. Do not hear it, o Duncan, the summons in-

terno che nel cielo ti chiama o nell'inferno!
fernal, That will lead you to Heav'n or Hell eternal!

(He enters the king's chamber.)

ALLEGRO ♩ = 100

30

(Lady Macbeth enters slowly.)

LADY REC.^{vo} (very softly throughout)

Regna il sonno su tutti... Oh, qual lamento!
All the world lies in slumber... Ah, sound of sorrow!

pp plaintively

46438

64

LADY: Risponde il gufo al suo lugubre addio!
The hooting howlet provides a mournful answer.

MAC. (from offstage): Chi v'ha?
Who's there?

LADY *Presto*: Ch'ei fosse di letargo uscito pria del colpo mortal!
What if in fear he had retreated without striking the blow?

col canto

MAC. (disheveled and staggering, brandishing a dagger) *as if choking*: Tutto è finito!
Ah... I have done it!

ALLEGRO ♩. = 88

MAC. (He moves close to Lady Macbeth and talks to her as if in a whisper.)

[31] Fatal mia donna! un murmure, com'io, non intendesti?
There was a murmur, a moan or sigh. Did you not hear a shrieking?

46438

65

L: Storna da questo il ciglio...
Why keep your eyes up - on them?

M: Oh vista or-ribile! oh vista or-ribile!
A sight too hor-ri-ble, too vile and hor-ri-ble!

sottovoce

M: Nel sonno udii che o-ra-vano i cortigiani, e: Dio
When steal-ing past the foot-men's bed I o-ver-heard them pray-ing.

sempre ne assista, ei dis-sero; Amen dir volli anch'io, ma la paro-la in-
"God may be with us" they soft-ly said. "A-men" I felt like say-ing. Yet, like a taunt, pro-

LADY: Folli-e! Folli-e!
How sil-ly! How sil-ly!

M: do-cile ge-lò sui labbri miei. Perchè, perchè ri-pe-tere quel-
vok-ing me, the "A-men" died a-way: As though a hand were chok-ing me. I

67

(as if laughing)
leggero

L: Fol-lie! follie che sperdono i primi rai del dì,— fol-li-e che sperdono i pri-mi rai del dì, folli-e! follie!
You fool! You fool! 'Twas nothing but your folly! 'Twill vanish at dawn.— Yes, fol-ly and fal-la-cy that van-ish at sun-rise to-day! Yes, fol-ly! Yes, fol-ly!

M: l'A-men non po-tei? Perchè, perchè, perchè non potei, perchè, perchè, perchè non potei, non po-tei, non po-tei?
could no long-er pray. Tell me: Why could I no long-er pray? Tell me: Why could I no long-er pray? Could not pray, could not pray?

morendo pp
pp
ppp

ANDANTINO ♪= 80
Long pause
33
MAC.
Al - lor que-sta vo-ce m'in-te-si nel pet-to: a-vrai per guan-cia-li sol
A voice spoke with-in me, fore-bod-ing and hol-low: "Your night-mare has start-ed. Be-
ANDANTINO ♪= 80
ve-pri, o Mac-bet - - - - - - to! Il son-no per sem-pre, Gla-
ware what will fol - - - - - - low! Be-ware, Thane of Gla-mis, for
mis, uc-ci-de - - - - - - sti! Non v'è che vi-gi-lia, Cau-
sleep have you mur - - - - - - dered! A-wake now, o Caw-dor, you
LADY
do-re, per te! Ma, dimmi, altra vo-ce non par-ti d'u-di-re? Sei
will sleep no more!" This voice which did haunt you, per-haps it did taunt you: "Mac-

L
va _ no, o Mac - bet - to, ma pri - vo d'ar - di - re; Gla -
beth's want of dar - ing falls foul of his bear - ing. This
p
pp
L
mis, a mez - z'o - pra va - cil - li, t'ar - re - sti; fan -
deed, stark and splen - did, can Gla - mis not end __ it? Your
L
ciul va _ ni - to - so, Cau - do - re, tu se'!
bite, no - ble Caw - dor, does not match your roar!"
MAC.
(with full voice)
Co - m'an - ge - li
A - ris - ing a -
34
Cantabile
M
d'i - ra, ven _ det - ta tuo _ nar - mi u - drò di Dun _ ca - no le
round me, the praise of his val - or Will sing of re - venge for the

LADY (aside) (under her breath)

Quell'animo trema, combatte, desante virtù.
How cravenly he trembles! How cowardly he stands and
King whom I slew.

lira... Chi mai lo direbbe l'invito che fu!
gazes! How little he resembles the hero I knew.

(softly)
Vendetta tuo
The praise of his

Chi mai lo direbbe l'invit to che fu!
How little he resembles the gallant man I knew.

narmi, com'angeli d'ira, udrò di Dun
valor, arising around me, Will sing of re-

71

L
M
quell'animo de - li - ra, quell'a - nimo de - li - ra, trema, de -
In fear he stands and trem - bles! How lit - tle he re - sem - bles the man I
tù
true,
u - drò le sue vir - tù.
his vengeance will pur - sue.
p
li - ra, chi mai lo di - reb - be, chi lo di - reb -
knew, this cow - ard here, who trem - bles! In fear he trem -
u - drò, u - drò le san - te sue vir - tù, le san -
My no - ble King so kind - ly and so true his ven -
36
f
pp
morendo
be l'invit - to che fu!
bles, the gal - lant man I knew!
te vir - tu.
geance will pur - sue!

LADY (to Macbeth)
ALL°. ♩. = 88
Il pu_gnal là ri_por_ta_te... le sue guar _ die insangui_
Near the guards, go, lay the dag-ger! Smear some blood o-ver their
f
pp
L
na_te... Che l'ac_cu _ sa in lor ri_cada.
cloth-ing! It is they who must seem guilt-y.
MAC.
Io co_ là? non
No, not I! I
M
pos _ so en_trar!
can - -not go!
LADY
Dammi il fer_ro.
Hand me the dag-ger!
(She wrests the dagger from Macbeth and rushes
into the king's chamber.)
p
(Loud knocks on the castle-gates.)
ff
MAC.
a piacere
O_gni ru_mo_re mi spa_venta!
Ah, ev-ery sound por-tends dis-as-ter!
(looking at his hands)
(terrified)
(with full voice)
Oh questa
Hands stained with
col canto

(Lady Macbeth returns.)

M: mano! non potrebbe l'Oceano queste mani a me lavar!
crimson! Could the vast and mighty ocean ever clean these hands of mine!

LADY: Ve'! le mani ho lorde anch'io; poco spruzzo, e monde son. L'opra anch'essa andrà in oblio...
Here, like yours, my hands are spotted! Yet a drop will wash them clean. Our good name will stay unblotted.

(Renewed knocking.)

MAC. Odi tu? raddoppia il suon!
Do you hear? What can this mean?

Long pause.

LADY *PRESTO ♩=120*
Vien! vien altrove, ogni sospetto rimoviam dall'uccisore; torna in
Come! Let us not arouse suspicion! Come away and do not worry! Let a-

L.
MAC.
te, fa cor, Mac-betto! non ti vinca in vil ti-mor. Oh po-tessi il mio de-
larm and pre-mo - ni-tion not af-fect you an-y-more! Could a shock of crime im-
pp
M
lit-to dalla mente cancel-lar! oh po-tessi, o re tra-fit-to, l'alto
mor-tal ev-er van-ish from my brain? Could a knock up-on the por-tal ev-er
pp
LADY
Vieni al-trove, ogni so-spet-to rimo-viam dall'ucci-
Let us not a-rouse sus-pi-cion! Come a-way and do not
M
sonno a te spez-zar! a te
wake my King a-gain! my King
p
L.
so-re; torna in te, fa cor, Mac-bet - to! non t'ac-cu - si un
wor-ry! Let a-larm and pre-mo-ni - tion not af-fect you
M
spezzar! potes-si il sonno, il sonno
a-gain! If on-ly this knock-ing could wak-en

cres.
L
vil ti - mor, ah non ti vin - ca un vil ti -
an - y - more! No, not af - fect you an - y -
M
spez - zar! po - tes - si, po - tes - sì il sonno a te spez -
King Dun - can! If on - ly this knock - ing could wak - en my King a -
38
cres.
pp
(Macbeth is
mor, ah! no, ah! no, vie - ni, vie - ni!
more! No more, no more! Hur - ry! Hur - ry!
- zar, a te spez - zar, pp spez - zar, spez - zar,
gain! Wake up my King! Wake up my King!
pp
pp
pulled away by Lady Macbeth.) (more and more distant)
vien! vien! vien! vien!
Come! Come! Come! Come!
a te spez - zar!
Wake up my King!
insensibilmente
morendo ed allarg.
ppp

FINALE 1

MACDUFF: Di destar lo per tempo il re m'impose;
The King had asked me to call on him by sun-rise.

e di gia tarda è l'ora. Qui m'attende te, o Banco.
I almost slipped the hour. Wait for me here, worthy Banquo!

(He enters the king's chamber.)

BANCO: Oh qual orrenda
Ah, what a night of

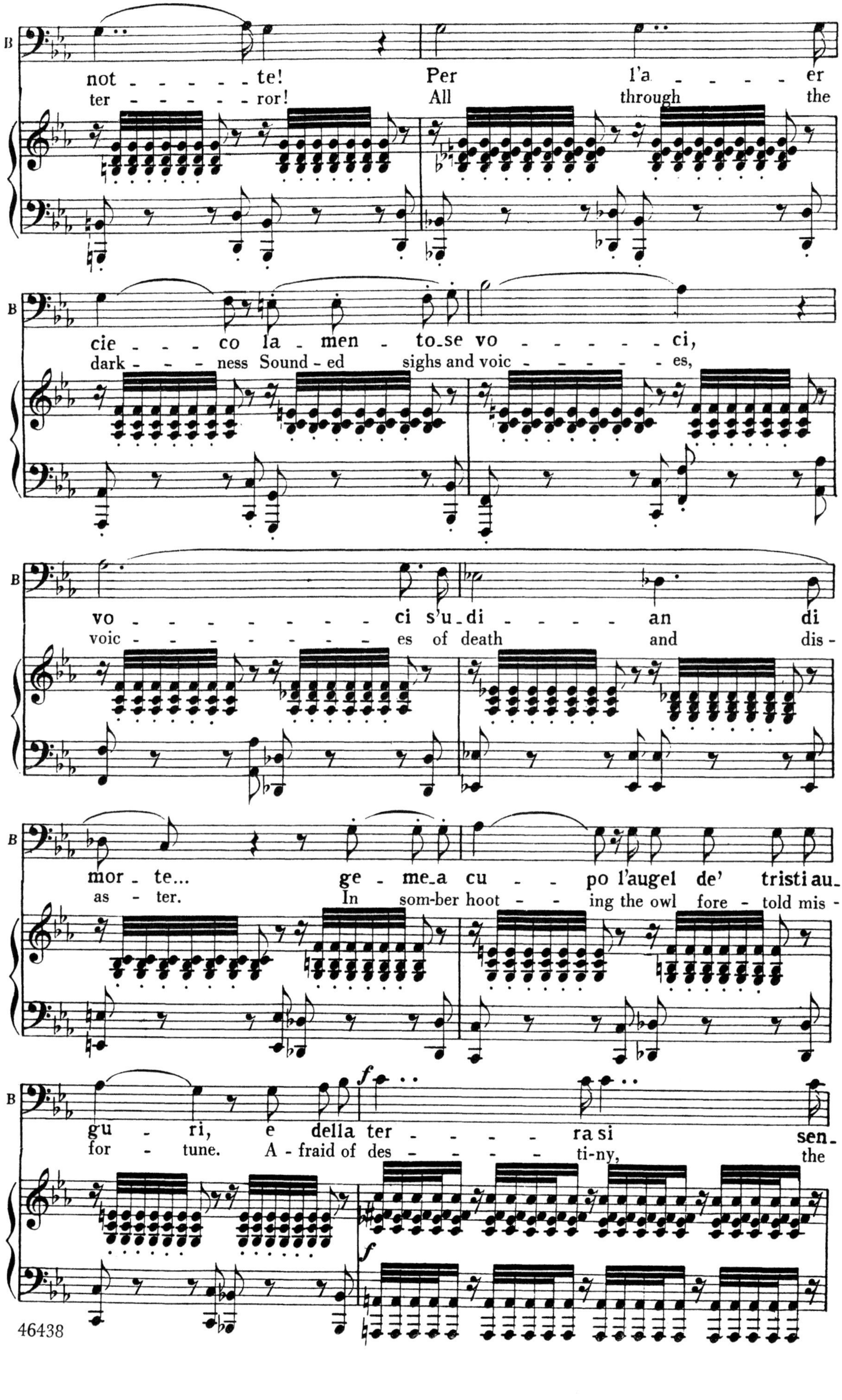
B
not - - - - - te! Per l'a - - - - - er
ter - - - - - - ror! All through the
cie - - co la - men - to_se vo - - - - - - ci,
dark - - - - ness Sound - ed sighs and voic - - - - - - es,
vo - - - - - - - - - ci s'u_di - - - - - an di
voic - - - - - - - - - es of death and dis -
mor - te... ge - me_a cu - - po l'augel de' tristi au_
as - ter. In som-ber hoot - - ing the owl fore - told mis -
gu - ri, e della ter - - - - - ra si sen_
for - tune. A - fraid of des - - - - - ti-ny, the
f
f

B
tì il tre-
earth seemed to
B
mo - - - - - - - - - - - - re!
trem - - - - - - - - - - - - ble.
ALL° AGITATO 𝅗𝅥=88 MACDUFF (reentering, in utmost agitation)
Or-
Oh,
ALL° AGITATO 𝅗𝅥=88
pp
p
M
ro-re! or-ro-re! or-ro-re!
hor-ror! Oh, hor-ror! Oh, hor-ror!
p
BANCO
Che avven-ne mai?
What is the mat-ter?
p
cresc.
MACDUFF (breathlessly)
Là... là den-tro con tem-
There in the cham-ber... go and
40
f
cresc.
p

pla - te voi stesso.... io dir nol pos - so!
see for your-selves... I can - not speak!

(Banquo rushes into the king's chamber.)

Corre - te, o-
A-wake! Come

là! Tut - ti ac-cor-re - te,
here! Hur-ry! All of you, come

(Macbeth, Lady Macbeth, her Lady-in-waiting, Malcolm, and others rush on stage.)

tutti! Oh de - litto! Oh de-
quick-ly! Blood and mur-der! Foul-est

lit - to! Oh tra - di - mento!
mur - der and be - tray-al!

81

L.
D
M
Mh.
B
la - te. Che se-guì di stra - no?
is it? Tell us what has hap - pened!
BANCO
(horrified)
È mor - to as-sas - - si-na-to il re Dun -
A mur - der - er has killed the King of
pp

ADAGIO ♩= 60
(Everyone is — or pretends to be — thunderstruck.)
LADY
fff
Schiudi, infer - no, la boc - ca ed in-ghiot-ti nel tuo
O - pen wide, might-y jaws of Dam-na - tion, O - pen
DAMA
MACDUFF
MALCOLM
MACBETH
BANCO
cano!
Scot-land!
Sop.
Ten.
Bassi
CORO
ADAGIO ♩= 60
ff
fff
Tutta forza

84

L
gno - to as - sassi - no e - se - cra - to le tue fiam - me, le tue
brow of the un - known as - sas - sin Pour your wrath. O Lord. in
D
gno - to as - sassi - no e - se - cra - to le tue fiam - me, le tue
brow of the un - known as - sas - sin Pour your wrath. O Lord. in
M.f
gno - to as - sassi - no e - se - cra - to le tue fiam - me, le tue
brow of the un - known as - sas - sin Pour your wrath. O Lord. and
M
gno - to as - sassi - no e - se - cra - to le tue fiam - me, le tue
brow of the un - known as - sas - sin Pour your wrath. O Lord. and
M.h
gno - to as - sassi - no e - se - cra - to le tue fiam - me, le tue
brow of the un - known as - sas - sin Pour your wrath, O Lord, and
B
gno - to as - sassi - no e - se - cra - to le tue fiam - me, le tue
brow of the un - known as - sas - sin Pour your wrath, O Lord. and
gno - to as - sassi - no e - se - cra - to le tue fiam - me, le tue
brow of the un - known as - sas - sin Pour your wrath, O Lord, and
gno - to as - sassi - no e - se - cra - to le tue fiam - me, le tue
brow of the un - known as - sas - sin Pour your wrath, O Lord, and
gno - to as - sassi - no e - se - cra - to le tue fiam - me, le tue
brow of the un - known as - sas - sin Pour your wrath, O Lord, and

86

87

Tu ne as-sisti, in te so-lo fi-dia-mo;
Aid us, God, in our or-deal stand be-side us!

Tu ne as-sisti, in te so-lo fi-dia-mo;
Aid us, God, in our or-deal stand be-side us!

Tu ne as-sisti, in te so-lo fi-dia-mo;
Aid us, God, in our or-deal stand be-side us!

ne-tri,   Tu ne as-sisti, in te solo, in te solo fi-
se-crets, Help us, God, in our sor-row stand firm-ly be-

Tu ne as-sisti, in te so-lo fi-dia-mo;
Aid us, God, in our or-deal stand be-side us!

ne-tri,   Tu ne as-sisti, in te solo, in te solo fi-
se-crets, Help us, God, in our sor-row stand firm-ly be-

ne-tri,   Tu ne as-sisti, in te solo, in te solo fi-
se-crets. Help us, God, in our sor-row stand firm-ly be-

ne-tri,   Tu ne as-sisti, in te solo, in te solo fi-
se-crets. Help us, God, in our sor-row stand firm-ly be-

L
da te lume, consiglio cer_chiamo
May Thy wis-dom en-light-en and guide us!
a squar_
Through the
D
da te lume, consiglio cer_chiamo
May Thy wis-dom en-light-en and guide us!
a squar_
Through the
Mf
da te lume, consiglio cer_chiamo
May Thy wis-dom en-light-en and guide us!
a squar_
Through the
M
pp
diamo;
side us!
da te lume, consiglio cerchiam
May Thy coun-sel con-sole us. O God!
Mh
da te lume, consiglio cer_chiamo
May Thy wis-dom en-light-en and guide us!
a squar_
Through the
B
pp
diamo;
side us!
da te lume, consiglio cerchiam
May Thy coun-sel con-sole us. O God!
pp
diamo;
side us!
da te lume, consiglio cerchiam
May Thy coun-sel con-sole us, O God!
pp
diamo;
side us!
da te lume, consiglio cerchiam
May Thy coun-sel con-sole us. O God!
pp
diamo;
side us!
da te lume, consiglio cerchiam
May Thy coun-sel con-sole us. O God!
pp

ff pp ppp morendo pp ppp sottovoce
lunga
L
ciar delle te_ne_bre, a squarciar il vel. O gran Di_o, che ne'cuori pe_
dark lead us on to light, to the truth, O Lord! O Re-deem-er, Thou who knowest our
D
ciar delle te_ne_bre, a squarciar il vel. O gran Di_o, che ne'cuori pe_
dark lead us on to light, to the truth, O Lord! O Re-deem-er, Thou who knowest our
Mf
ciar delle te_ne_bre, a squarciar il vel. O gran Di_o, che ne'cuori pe_
dark lead us on to light, to the truth, O Lord! O Re-deem-er, Thou who knowest our
M
delle te_ne_bre, a squarciar il vel. O gran Di_o, che ne'cuori pe_
Lead us on to light, to the truth, O Lord! O Re-deem-er, Thou who knowest our
Mh
ciar delle te_ne_bre, a squarciar il vel. O gran Di_o, che ne'cuori pe_
dark lead us on to light, to the truth, O Lord! O Re-deem-er, Thou who knowest our
B
delle te_ne_bre, a squarciar il vel. O gran Di_o, che ne'cuori pe_
Lead us on to light, to the truth, O Lord! O Re-deem-er, Thou who knowest our
delle te_ne_bre, a squarciar il vel.
Lead us on to light, to the truth, O Lord!
delle te_ne_bre, a squarciar il vel.
Lead us on to light, to the truth, O Lord!
delle te_ne_bre, a squarciar il vel.
Lead us on to light, to the truth, O Lord!
morendo pp ppp p

netri, Tu ne assisti, in te solo fidiamo, a squar-
secrets, Stand beside us in this hour of misfortune! May Thy

da te lume cer-
Guide us on through the

O gran Dio!
O Redeemer!

O gran Dio!
O Redeemer!

(sharp cut-off)
dim.
L
ciа - re il ve - - lo, a squar - ciar, a squarciar, a squar-
coun - sel guide us through the night, Through the dark of the
D
cia - re il ve - - lo, a squar - ciar, a squarciar, a squar-
coun - sel guide us through the night, Through the dark of the
Mf
cia - re il ve - - lo, a squar - ciar, a squarciar, a squar-
coun - sel guide us through the night, Through the dark of the
M
cia - re il ve - - lo, a squar - ciar, a squarciar, a squar-
coun - sel guide us through the night, Through the dark of the
Mh
chiam a squarciar, a squar - ciar, a squarciar, a squar-
night, Guide us on through the night, Through the dark of the
B
chiam a squarciar, a squar - ciar, a squarciar, a squar-
night, Guide us on through the night, Through the dark of the
Il ve - - lo a squar - ciar,
Oh, guide us through the night,
Il ve - - lo a squar - ciar,
Oh, guide us through the night,
Il ve - - lo a squar - ciar,
Oh, guide us through the night,

GRANDIOSO
L
ciar delle te-nebre, a squarcia - re il vel. L'i - ra
night lead us on-ward To the light, O Lord! All con-
D
ciar delle te-nebre, a squarcia - re il vel. L'i - ra
night lead us on-ward To the light, O Lord! All con-
Mf
ciar delle te-nebre, a squarciar, squarciare il vel. L'i - ra
night lead us on-ward To the light of truth, O Lord! All con-
M
ciar delle te-nebre, a squarciar, squarciare il vel. L'i - ra
night lead us on-ward To the light of truth, O Lord! All con-
Mh
ciar delle te-nebre, a squarciar, squarciare il vel. L'i - ra
night lead us on-ward To the light of truth, O Lord! All con-
B
ciar delle te-nebre, a squarciar, squarciare il vel. L'i - ra
night lead us on-ward To the light of truth, O Lord! All con-
GRANDIOSO
squarciar, squarciare il vel. L'i - ra
To light and truth, O Lord! All con-
squarciar, squarciare il vel. L'i - ra
To light and truth, O Lord! All con-
squarciar, squarciare il vel. L'i - ra
To light and truth, O Lord! All con-
GRANDIOSO
43

L
tu - - a, l'i - ra tu - - a for - mi -
sum - - ing, ev - er doom - - ing, may the
D
tu - - a, l'i - ra tu - - a for - mi -
sum - - ing, ev - er doom - - ing, may the
Mf
tu - - a, l'i - ra tu - - a for - mi -
sum - - ing, ev - er doom - - ing, may the
M
tu - - a, l'i - ra tu - - a for - mi -
sum - - ing, ev - er doom - - ing, may the
Mh
tu - - a, l'i - ra tu - - a for - mi -
sum - - ing, ev - er doom - - ing, may the
B
tu - - a, l'i - ra tu - - a for - mi -
sum - - ing, ev - er doom - - ing, may the
tu - - a, l'i - ra tu - - a for - mi -
sum - - ing, ev - er doom - - ing, may the
tu - - a, l'i - ra tu - - a for - mi -
sum - - ing, ev - er doom - - ing, may the
tu - - a, l'i - ra tu - - a for - mi -
sum - - ing, ev - er doom - - ing, may the

da - bi - le   e____ pron - - ta   col - ga
wrath of God   fall   up - on   him!   May the

96

tal, fa_tal pu_ni_tor; e vi
mark of Cain on his brow! Mark the

tal, fa_tal pu_ni_tor;
mark of Cain on his brow!

tal, fa_tal pu_ni_tor; e vi
mark of Cain on his brow! Mark the

tal, fa_tal pu_ni_tor;
mark of Cain on his brow!

tal, fa_tal pu_ni_tor, e vi stam_pa
mark of Cain on his brow! O, Cre-a - tor,

tal, fa_tal pu_ni_tor; e vi stam_pa
mark of Cain on his brow! O, Cre-a - tor,

tal, fa_tal pu_ni_tor;
mark of Cain on his brow!

tal, fa_tal pu_ni_tor;
mark of Cain on his brow!

tal, fa_tal pu_ni_tor;
mark of Cain on his brow!

L
cres.
stam - - - - - pa sul vol - - - - - - to l'im-
trai - - - - - tor, Cre-a - - - - - - tor, the
D
fa - - - - - - - - - - tal pu-ni-
Pun - - - - - - - - - - ish, brand the
M!
stam - - - - - pa sul vol - - - - - - to l'im-
trai - - - - - tor, Cre-a - - - - - - tor, the
M
M!
e vi stam - pa sul vol - to l'im-
brand the trai - tor, mark the mon - ster, the
B
e vi stam - pa sul vol - to l'im-
brand the trai - tor, mark the mon - ster, the
cresc.

L
pron - ta___ che stam - pa - sti, stampa - sti, stam-
mur - d'rer, the mon - ster for - ev - er and ev - er! Re-
D
tor, che stam - pa - sti, stampa - sti, stam-
mon - - - ster for - ev - er and ev - er! Re-
Mf
pron - ta___ che stam - pa - sti, stampa - sti, stam-
mur - d'rer, the mon - ster for - ev - er and ev - er! Re-
M
che stam - - - pa - - - sti sul
Mark the trai - - - - tor by
Mh
pron - - ta che stam - pa - - - - sti sul
mur - - der-er for - ev - - - - er by
B
pron - - ta che stam - pa - - - - sti sul
mur - - der-er for - ev - - - - er by
che stam - - - pa - - - sti sul
Mark the trai - - - tor by
che stam - - - pa - - - sti sul
Mark the trai - - - tor by
che stam - - - pa - - - sti sul
Mark the trai - - - tor by
44

pa-sti sul pri-mo uc-ci-sor, col-ga
veal him by brand-ing his brow! May the

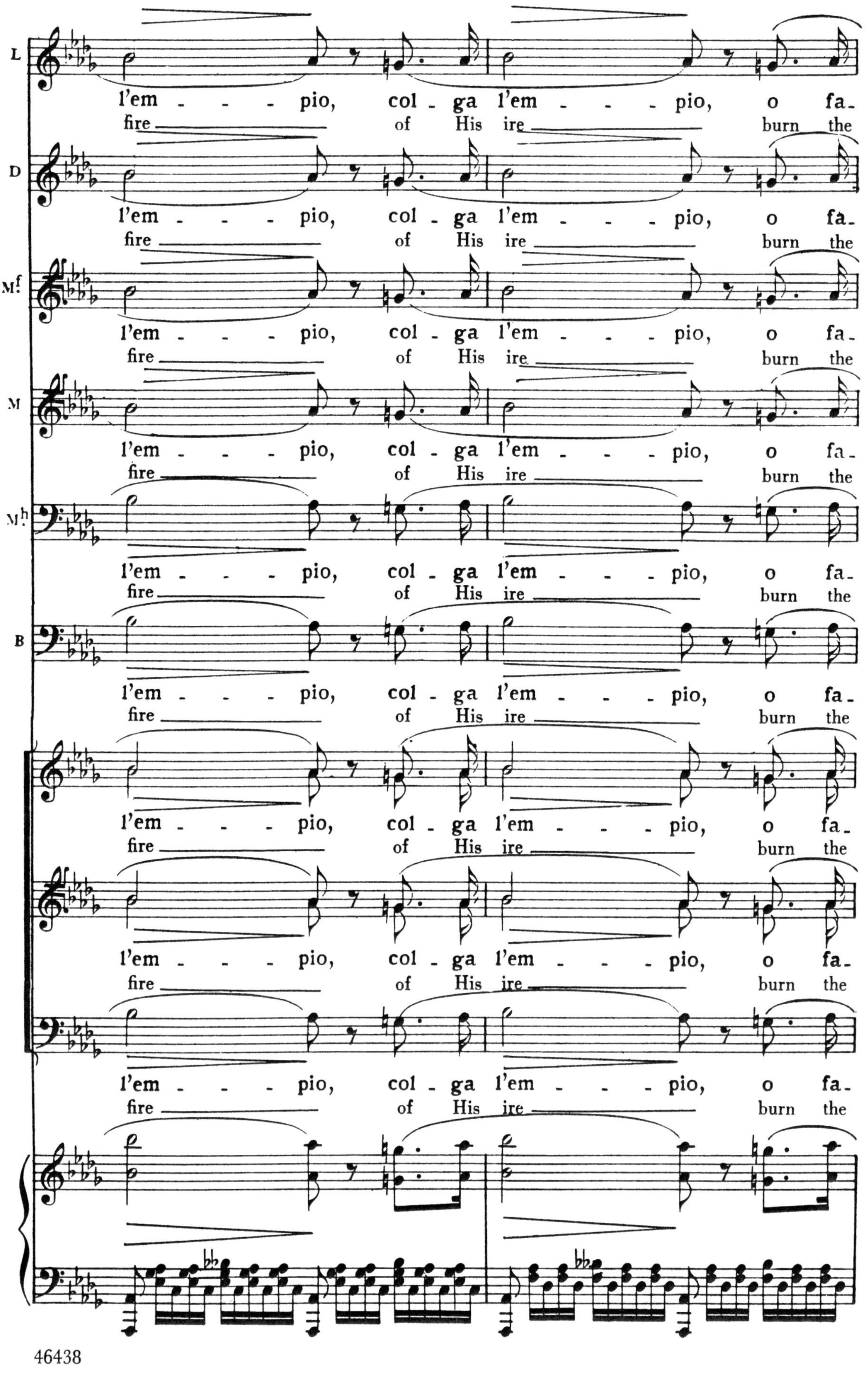
L
l'em - - - pio, col - ga l'em - - - pio, o fa-
fire of His ire burn the
D
l'em - - - pio, col - ga l'em - - - pio, o fa-
fire of His ire burn the
Mf
l'em - - - pio, col - ga l'em - - - pio, o fa-
fire of His ire burn the
M
l'em - - - pio, col - ga l'em - - - pio, o fa-
fire of His ire burn the
Mh
l'em - - - pio, col - ga l'em - - - pio, o fa-
fire of His ire burn the
B
l'em - - - pio, col - ga l'em - - - pio, o fa-
fire of His ire burn the
l'em - - - pio, col - ga l'em - - - pio, o fa-
fire of His ire burn the
l'em - - - pio, col - ga l'em - - - pio, o fa-
fire of His ire burn the
l'em - - - pio, col - ga l'em - - - pio, o fa-
fire of His ire burn the

tal, fa - tal pu - ni - tor; e vi stam - pa
mark of Cain on his brow! O Cre-a - tor, Mark the

103

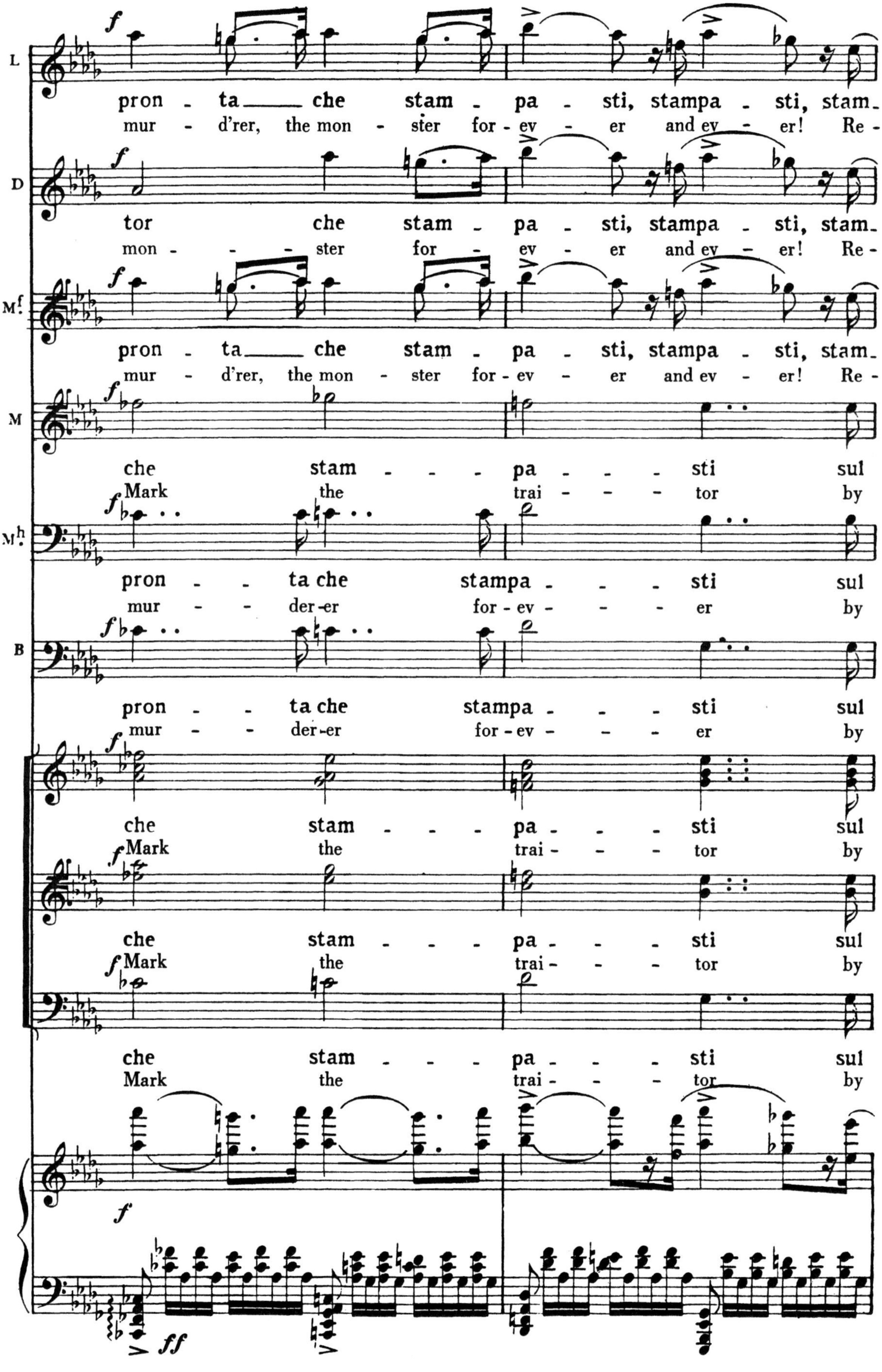

ALLEGRO 𝅗𝅥 = 92
L
pa - sti sul pri - mo uc - ci - sor, sul pri - mo ucci -
veal him by brand - ing his brow! The wrath of the
D
pa - sti sul pri - mo uc - ci - sor, sul pri - mo ucci -
veal him by brand - ing his brow! The wrath of the
M!
pa - sti sul pri - mo uc - ci - sor, sul pri - mo ucci -
veal him by brand - ing his brow! The wrath of the
M
pri - - mo uc - ci - sor, sul pri - mo ucci -
brand - - - ing his brow! The wrath of the
M!
pri - - mo uc - - ci - sor, sul pri - mo ucci -
brand - - - ing his brow! The wrath of the
B
pri - - mo uc - - ci - sor, sul pri - mo ucci -
brand - - - ing his brow! The wrath of the
ALLEGRO 𝅗𝅥 = 92
pri - - mo uc - - ci - sor, sul pri - mo ucci -
brand - - - ing his brow! The wrath of the
pri - - mo uc - ci - sor, sul pri - mo ucci -
brand - - - ing his brow! The wrath of the
pri - - mo uc - - ci - sor, sul pri - mo ucci -
brand - - - ing his brow! The wrath of the
ALLEGRO 𝅗𝅥 = 92
ff tutta forza

106

107

L
sor, sul pri - mo ucci - sor— che stampa-sti, stam -
Lord shall fall on the kill-er, And the blood-mark of
D
sor, sul pri - mo ucci - sor— che stampa-sti, stam -
Lord shall fall on the kill-er, And the blood-mark of
Mf
sor, sul pri - mo ucci - sor— che stampa-sti,— stam -
Lord shall fall on the kill-er, And the blood-mark— of
M
sor, sul pri - mo ucci - sor— che stampa-sti,— stam -
Lord shall fall on the kill-er, And the blood-mark— of
Mh
sor, sul pri - mo ucci - sor— che stampa-sti, stam -
Lord shall fall on the kill-er, And the blood-mark of
B
sor, sul pri - mo ucci - sor— che stampa-sti,— stam -
Lord shall fall on the kill-er, And the blood-mark— of
sor, sul pri - mo ucci - sor— che stampa-sti, stam -
Lord shall fall on the kill-er, And the blood-mark of
sor, sul pri - mo ucci - sor— che stampa-sti,— stam -
Lord shall fall on the kill-er, And the blood-mark— of
sor, sul pri - mo ucci - sor— che stampa-sti,— stam -
Lord shall fall on the kill-er, And the blood-mark— of

109

110

End of Act I

ACT II

Scene 1

A Room in the Castle.

(Macbeth, deep in thought, is joined by Lady Macbeth.)

LADY *REC.vo*

Perchè mi sfuggi, e fiso ognor ti veggo in un pensier profondo? Il fatto è irreparabile! Veraci parlâr le maliarde, e re tu sei! Il figlio di Duncan, per l'improvvisa sua fuga in Inghilterra, parricida fu detto, e vuoto il soglio a te lasciò.

Why do you shun me, your mien depressed and somber, as in the throes of worry? What's done is done! Remember this! And just as the witches foretold you, you're King of Scotland. while Duncan's son, the prince, who fled to England, has by his swift departure aroused suspicion and, by absconding, left you the throne.

MACBETH

Ma le spirtali donne Banco padre di regi han profe-
And yet the ghostly women have called Banquo a father of royal

M
ta_to...
children!
Dunque i suoi fi_gli re_gne_ran?
One day his sons would thus be kings.
ff
p
tr
LADY
M
Egli e suo
They are still
Dunca_no per co_stor sa_rà spen - - to?
Was it for them that Dun-can was mur - - dered?
L
fi_glio vi_vono,è ver...
liv-ing, he and his son...
Ah sì, non l'hanno!
In-deed, they shall not!
Ma vi_ta immor_ta_le non hanno...
How-ev-er, they shall not be im-mor-tal...
Dove? Quando?
Where? When?
For_za è che scor_ra un al_tro sangue,o don - na!
So, once a-gain our For-tune calls for blood - shed.
Al ve_
Ere the
f

(softly and very slowly)

L: Immo-to sa-rai tu nel tuo di - se - gno?
Your pur-pose and re - solve, will they not fail you?

M: nir di que-sta not-te.
dawn will rise to - mor-row.

(firmly) ... *(off)*

M: Ban - co! l'e-ter-ni - tà ___ t'apre il suo re - gno.
Ban - quo! Once and for all, ___ may Heav-en hail ___ you!

AND.!º SOST.!º

1 ALL.º MODERATO ♩ = 100

116

LADY *legato e cupo*

La luce langue, il faro spegnesi
Sun, warm and tender, born of eternity,

ch'eterno scorrere per gl'ampi cieli!
Soon will your splendor bow in surrender.

Notte desiata, provvida veli
Dark, then, and clouded, night will have shrouded

la man colpevole che ferirà.
Him by whose dagger the victim will fall.

46438

(almost spoken)
Nuovo de-lit-to!
An-oth-er mur-der?

nuovo de-litto! È neces-sa-rio! è neces-
An-oth-er mur-der? For-tune com-mands it! For-tune com-

sa-rio! com-pier-si deb-be l'o-pra fa-
mands it! We must a-chieve it once we con-

ta-le, compiersi debbe, compiersi debbe l'opra fa-ta-le.
ceive it: Mean and ma-li-cious, e-vil and vi-cious, we can-not leave it.

ANDANTE SOS.to ♩ = 80
lunga a piacere
L
Ai trapas_sa_ti regnar non ca_le; a loro un requiem, l'e_terni_tà!
Those who've de-part-ed care not for glo-ry: Theirs be a Req-ui-em once and for all!
pp
ANDANTE SOS.to ♩ = 80
pp
pp
ALL.o VIVO 𝅗𝅥 = 84
(ecstatically)
O volut_tà del soglio! o scettro, o
Oh, to en-joy such rap-ture! A throne is
ALL.o VIVO 𝅗𝅥 = 84
p
f col canto
p
pp
scettro, alfin sei mio. O ogni mortal de_sì_o_ta_ce,
mine, a crown and sceptre! On - - - to my roy-al des-ti-ny no
f
p
p
a tempo
(with a little tremor of pleasure and excitement in the voice)
3
ta_ce e s'acqueta in te. O vo_lut_tà, o vo_lut_tà del
qualm shall now de-fy! Ec-sta-sy, de-light, oh joy sub-lime and
f
a tempo
il più piano possibile
ppp

so- glio! o scet- tro, al fin sei mi-
splen- did: A roy- al crown, a scep- tre, a

o, sei mi- o. O gni mor- tal, o-
throne are mine at last! Free of doubt and fear, I

gni mortal de- si- o ta- ce e s'ac- que- ta, s'acque- ta in
rise, as Fate in- tend- ed, On- ward to my glo- ry no qualm shall de-

te! Ca- drà fra po- co e
ny! To- night, this eve- ning, a

L
sa - nime chi fu predet - to Re, ca -
dy - nas-ty to be will fall and die, At
cresc.
poco
poco
4
ff
L
drà, ca - drà chi fu pre - det - to Re, ca - drà, ca -
last to - night a dy - nas - ty will die! To - night, tonight at
L
drà chi fu predetto Re, cadrà chi fu predet - to
last a dy - nas-ty will die, To-night a dy - nas-ty will
J
Re, ca - drà.
die, will die!
8

Scene 2

A Park near Macbeth's Castle.

Chorus of Cutthroats

Tenori
(Two groups of cutthroats are meeting.)
CORO
Bassi
p
Chi v'im - po - se u - nir - vi a noi?
Who has told you to come here?
Fu Mac - bet - to...
pp King Mac - beth did
5
Ed a che far?
He did? And why?
Deg - giam
Ban - quo's
Ban - co tru - ci - dar.
end, it seems, is near.
Quan - do?
Is it?
Do - ve?
Tru - ly?
pp

Insiem con voi. Con suo figlio ei qui ver-rà.
He has to die. With his son he's on his way.

Rimane-te, or bene sta.
We will help you. You may stay.

sotto voce ed assai staccato

Sparve il sol, la notte or re-gni scel-le-rata, insanguina
Day is dy-ing and the night will fall, Dark and se-cre-cy will cov-er

Sparve il sol, la notte or re-gni scel-le-rata, insanguina
Day is dy-ing and the night will fall, Dark and se-cre-cy will cov-er

123

46438

ta; cie- ca notte, affretta e spe- gni o- gni lume in terra, in ciel, in
all. Now the wick-ed wolf will leave his lair. May the in-no-cent be-ware ev-ery-

ciel. L'ora è presso, or n'occultia- - mo, nel si- lenzio lo aspettia- -
where! On- ly we still have a job to do: Kings have hired us, and har-lots,

mo. Tre- ma, Banco! nel tuo fian- - co sta la punta del coltel, del col-
too! Care-ful, Ban-quo, for be-tray- al's rife. You will short-ly lose your life to a

tel! Trema, Banco! Trema, Banco! nel tuo fianco sta la punta del col_tel!
knife. Trem-ble, Ban-quo! Trem-ble, Ban-quo! For your life will be the tar-get of a knife!

tel! Trema, Banco! Trema, Banco! nel tuo fianco sta la punta del col_tel!
knife. Trem-ble, Ban-quo! Trem-ble, Ban-quo! For your life will be the tar-get of a knife!

sotto voce ed assai staccato

Spar_ve il sol, la notte or re_
Hushed and hid-den by the black of

Spar_ve il sol, la notte or re_
Hushed and hid-den by the black of

staccato assai

gni scel_le_rata, insanguina_ta; cie_ca
night, Noth-ing tells on us, no sound or light. Here we

gni scel_le_rata, insanguina_ta; cie_ca
night, Noth-ing tells on us, no sound or light. Here we

pp
notte, affretta e spe - - gni o - gni lume in terra, in ciel, in
ply our trade with craft - y skill: All the world is keep-ing still while we
pp
notte, affretta e spe - - gni o - gni lume in terra, in ciel, in
ply our trade with craft - y skill: All the world is keep-ing still while we
pp
ppp
ciel. L'o - ra è presso, or n'occultia - - mo, nel si -
kill. Fast and sure - ly will the deed be done. Ban - quo's
ppp
ciel. L'o - ra è presso, or n'occultia - - mo, nel si -
kill. Fast and sure - ly will the deed be done. Ban - quo's
lenzio lo aspettia - - mo. Tre - ma, Banco! nel tuo fian - -
eyes will nev - er see the sun. Swift and si - lent, we will send the
lenzio lo aspettia - - mo. Tre - ma, Banco! nel tuo fian - -
eyes will nev - er see the sun. Swift and si - lent, we will send the

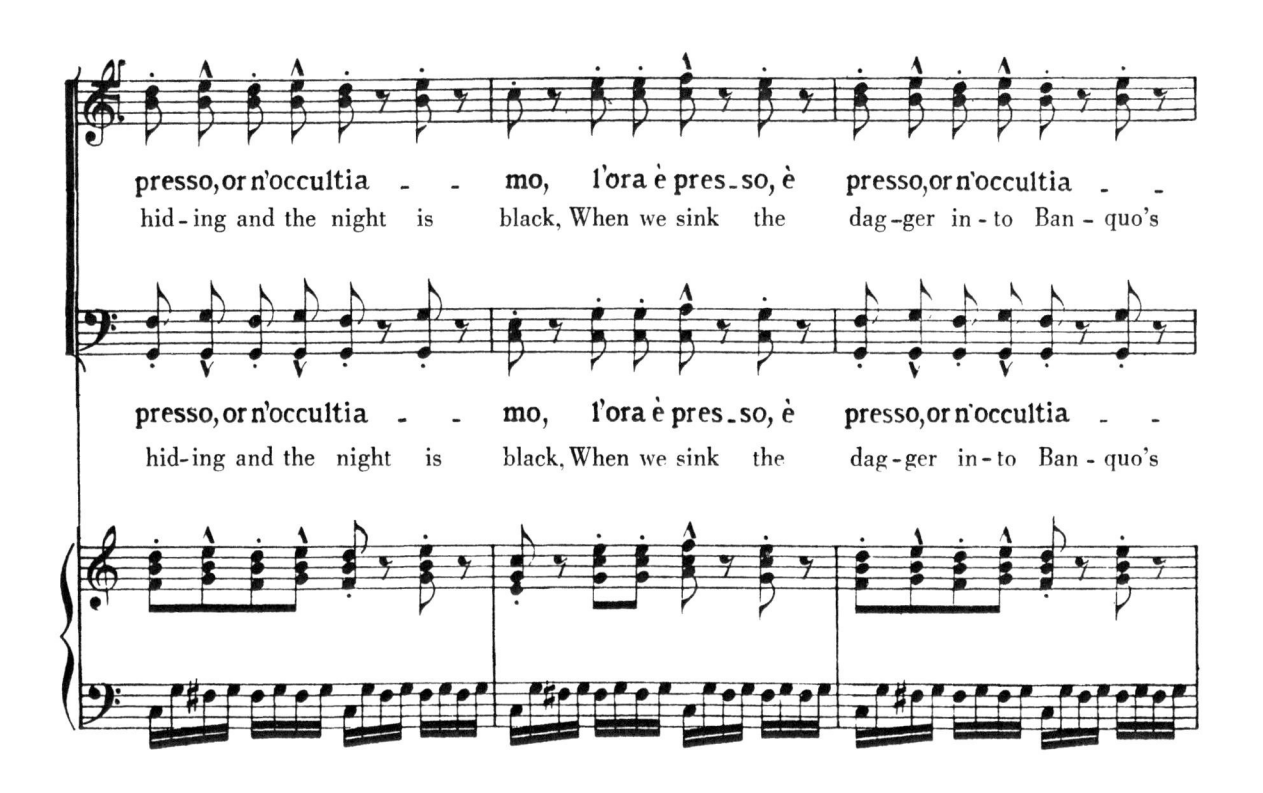

co- sta la punta del coltel, del coltel! L'ora è presso, è
dart, Plunge a dagger in his heart and depart. Ev-ery star is

co- sta la punta del coltel, del coltel! L'ora è presso, è
dart, Plunge a dagger in his heart and depart. Ev-ery star is

presso, or n'occultia- - -mo, l'ora è presso, è presso, or n'occultia- -
hid-ing and the night is black, When we sink the dag-ger in-to Ban-quo's

presso, or n'occultia- - -mo, l'ora è presso, è presso, or n'occultia- -
hid-ing and the night is black, When we sink the dag-ger in-to Ban-quo's

mo. Trema Banco! Tre - ma. Trema, Banco! Tre - ma.
back! Trem-ble, Ban-quo! Meet your death! Trem-ble, Ban-quo! Greet Mac-beth!

mo. Trema, Banco! Tre - ma. Trema, Banco! Tre - ma.
back! Trem-ble, Ban-quo! Meet your death! Trem-ble, Ban-quo! Greet Mac - beth!

(withdrawing) *morendo*

Nel si-lenzio lo aspet-tiam. Nel si-lenzio lo aspet-tiam.
As for now we bet-ter hide, Bet-ter hide and draw a - side!

Nel si-lenzio lo aspet-tiam. Nel si-lenzio lo aspet-tiam.
As for now we bet-ter hide, Bet-ter hide and draw a - side!

(They withdraw into hiding.)

(Enter Banquo and his son, Fleance.)

BANCO — REC.^{vo}

Studia il passo, o mio figlio! u-sciam da queste te-nèbre... un senso i-gno-to na-scer mi sen-to in pet-to pien di tri-sto pre-sa-gio e di so-spet-to.

Come, my son, mind your foot-steps! Let's flee this caul-dron of dark-ness! Some sense of dan-ger, some fear or in-tu-i-tion fills my heart with fore-bod-ing and with sus-pi-cion.

ADAGIO ♩=56
B
Co_me dal ciel pre_ci _ pita l'ombra più sem_pre o_
Ah, on this night of reck - on-ing Ghosts of the past con -
ADAGIO ♩=56
mf
scu _ ra! In notteugual tra_fis_se_ro Dun_ca _ _ _ _ no,il mio si
found me: On such a night as this they killed my King, my no-ble
ff
9
gnor. Mil _ le af _ fanno _ _ se im_
Lord. Out of the dark come
p
ma _ gi _ ni m'an_nun _ cia _ no sven _ tu _ ra,
beck - on - ing, a - ris - ing all a - round me.

e il mio pensie - ro in_gom - bra - no di
Mem' - ries of days now far and gone, and

lar - ve e_ di_ ter - ror, di terror,
dreams of_ crime and_ fi - nal re-ward.

e il mio pensie - ro in_gom - bra - no di lar - ve, di_
Out of the dark - ness a-round me rise the mem' - ries of the

lar - ve e di ter - ror, il mio pen_siero ingom_bra -
night they killed my Lord. Un-ho - ly mem'-ry of the

B
no di ter - ror, il mio pensiero ingombra -
time they slew my Lord! When will this vile and fear-some
pp
ff
B
no di ter - ror, ingom - bra -
crime find its re - ward its due re -
pp
pp
pp
B
ppp
no di ter - ror, e di terror, e di ter -
ward, its re - ward? Ah, when will time a-venge my
ff (Banquo and Fleance wander off into the park.)
B
ror.
Lord?
11
ff
ppp

133

FINALE 2

The Great Hall of the Castle
A banquet table is set.
Macbeth, Lady Macbeth, Macduff, the Lady-in-waiting, Guests, etc.

All⁰. Brillante ♩ = 144

MACBETH
Voi pur sal-vete, no-bilis-simi si-gno - - ri!
My thanes and nobles, hail and welcome on your en - - try!
Sop.
Sal-ve, o re!
Hail, o King!
Ten.
Sal-ve, o re!
Hail, o King!
Bassi
Sal-ve, o re!
Hail, o King!
LADY
Ri - ce-vete la mer-ce' de' vo - stri o-
Hail and welcome to you, Sirs, and La - - dies of
Sal - ve, o donna!
Hail, my La-dy!
Sal - ve, o donna!
Hail, my La-dy!
Sal - ve, o donna!
Hail, my La-dy!

MACB. Pren-da ciascun l'or-re-vole seggio al suo grado e-
no-ri.
gen-try! Now if it please, you gen-tle-men, let us be-gin the

let-to! Pa-go son io d'ac-co-gliere ta-li o-spi-ti a ban-
par-ty! Nev-er be-fore I've host-ed here a crowd so proud and

chet-to. La mia consorte as-si-dasi nel tro-no a lei sor-
heart-y. My La-dy will not think it wrong, that, ere she start the

ti-to, ma pria le piaccia un brin-disi scio-gliere a vo-stro o-
din-ner. She of-fer us a drink-ing-song, rais-ing our spir-its

137

138

139

L
sde - gni, fol - leg - gi e re - gni qui so - lo a - mor.
suf - fer? What wine has to of - fer we all will a - dore.
17
L
a - mor. Gu - stiamo il bal - samo d'o - gni fe - ri - ta, che
A - dore the price - less rem - e - dy, po - tent and pleas - ing, so
pp
L
nuo - va vi - ta ri - - do - na al cor Cac - ciam le tor - bi - de
gen - tly eas - ing the cares of yore. A - way with mis - er - y,
L
cu - re dal pet - to; nasca il di - let - to, muo - ia il do -
heart - ache, and sor - row: Think of to - mor - row and wor - ry no

141

142

143

144

nasca il di - let - to, muo - ia il do lor, ah muoia, muo -
Think of to - mor-row and wor - ry no more! Not ev - er more, ah!

nasca il di - let - to, muo - ia il do = lor, muoia il do -
Think of to - mor-row and wor - ry no more! We'll pine no

nasca il di - let - to, muo - ia il do - lor, muoia il do -
Think of to - mor-row and wor - ry no more! We'll pine no

nasca il di - let - to, muo - ia il do - lor, muoia il do -
Think of to - mor-row and wor - ry no more! We'll pine no

na - sca il di - let - to, muo - ia il do - lor, muoia il do -
Think of to - mor-row and wor - ry no more! We'll pine no

na - sca il di - let - to, muo - ia il do - lor, muoia il do -
Think of to - mor-row and wor - ry no more! We'll pine no

46438

145

146

lor, muoia il do - lor, muoia il do - lor.
more! We will not wor-ry an - y - more!

(One of the cutthroats appears in the doorway. Approaching him
MACBETH stealthily, Macbeth whispers to him.)

Tu di san - gue hai brut - to il
On your hands, this blood whose

46438

(overjoyed)
M
vol - to.
is it?
Il ve - ro a-scol - to?
You are quite cer - tain?
Ma il
But his
SICARIO
sotto voce
E di Banco.
It is Ban-quo's.
Sì.
Yes.
M
fi-glio?
son?
Cielo!
Heav-ens!
ma Ban - co?
and Ban - quo?
S
Ne sfug-gì!
His son has fled.
E - gli mo-rì.
Ban - quo is dead.
(Macbeth dismisses the cutthroat.)
tr
morendo
ALL° COME PRIMA ♩ = 144
20
p

LADY (drawing closer to Macbeth, addresses him)

Che ti sco - sta, o re mio spo - so, dal - la gio - ia del ban - chet - to?
Why with-draw, my hus - band roy - al, from this feast of joy and beau - ty?

MACBETH

Banco fal - la, il va - lo - ro - so chiu - de - reb - be il ser - to e - let - to a quan -
The most loy - al of the loy - al did for once for - sake his du - ty: Where is

149

LADY
Che par - li?
What is it?
DAMA
Che par - li?
What is it?
MACDUFF
Che par - li?
What is it?
(to Banquo's ghost)
M
fe - ce? Non dir - - mi ch'io
did this? You can - not say I
Che par - li?
What is it?
Che par - li?
What is it?
C O R O
Che par - li?
What is it?
pp
f
cupo
pp
M
fos-si! le cioc - che cru - en - to non scuoter-mi in -
did it! Then why are you shak - ing your gor-y locks at
pp
f

151

uo - mo voi sie - te?) Lo so - no ed au - da - ce s'io
call your-self a man?— A man, yes in-deed, a cou-

guar - - do tal co - sa che al de - - mo - ne
ra - - geous and bold one Who dares to be-

stes - - so fa - reb - - be spa - ven - to... là...
hold what would fright - - en a Dev - il... There...

là... là... là... no! rav - vi - si? là...
there... there... there! Can't you see it there?

(To Banquo's ghost)

Oh, poi che le chiome scrol_lar t'è con_ces_so, favel_la! il se_pol_cro può ren_der gli uc_ci_si? può ren_der, può ren_der gli uc_ci_si, la tom_ba può ren_der gli uc_

And you who are a_ble to sit at my ta_ble, now tell me: If you're killed, can the bone_yard re_lease you? Can dead men re_turn to the liv_ing, the bur_ied ones come back to haunt and

LADY
POCO PIÙ LENTO 𝅗𝅥=60
(under her breath, to Macbeth)
Voi sie_te de_mente!
You must be de-ment-ed!
M
(The ghost disappears.)
ci - si, fa_vel - la!
tease_ us? Pray tell_ me!
Que_
My
POCO PIU LENTO 𝅗𝅥=60
L
(calming him)
Se - de - te, mio spo - so! O - gn'o - spi - te è
Re - gain your com - po - sure! Your guests are un -
st'occhi l'han vi_sto...
eyes have be - held him.
tri - sto. Sve_glia - tè la gio - ia!
eas - y. Re - store us to gaiet - y!
(calmly)
Cia_scun mi per_do - ni! Il
My no - bles, for-give me! Re -

155

letto, muoia il dolor. Da noi s'involino
af - ter, let us ig - nore! Fare-well, an - xi - e - ty!

gli o-die gli sdegni, folleggi e regni qui solo a-
Why should we suf-fer? What wine has to of-fer we all will a-

mor, amor. Gustiamo il balsamo d'ogni fe-
dore... A-dore the price-less rem-e-dy, po-tent and

rita, che nuova vita ridona al cor. Vuo tiam per
pleas-ing, so gently eas-ing the cares of yore. A toast to

l'inclito Banco i bicchieri! fior de' guerrieri, di Scozia onor.
Banquo, Scotsman victorious! Long live his glory in peace and in war!

DAMA
Vuotiam per l'inclito Banco i bicchieri!
A toast to Banquo, Scotsman victorious!

MACD.
Vuotiam per l'inclito Banco i bicchieri!
A toast to Banquo, Scotsman victorious!

Vuotiam per l'inclito Banco i bicchieri!
A toast to Banquo, Scotsman victorious!

Vuotiam per l'inclito Banco i bicchieri!
A toast to Banquo, Scotsman victorious!

Vuotiam per l'inclito Banco i bicchieri!
A toast to Banquo, Scotsman victorious!

158

L
nor, di_Scozia o _ nor, o - - - - nor, o - - - - - - -
_ - In_peace and_war Ah, in
D
nor, di Sco_zia o _ nor, di Sco_zia o _ nor, di Scozia o_
soar In peace and war, May Ban - quo's fame for-ev - er
M.
nor, di Sco_zia o _ nor, di Sco_zia o _ nor, di Scozia o_
soar In peace and war, May Ban - quo's fame for-ev - er
nor, di Sco_zia o _ nor, di Sco_zia o _ nor, di Scozia o_
soar In peace and war, May Ban - quo's fame for-ev - er
nor di Sco_zia o _ nor, di Sco_zia o _ nor, di Scozia o_
soar In peace and war, May Ban - quo's fame for- ev - er
nor, di Sco_zia o _ nor, di Sco_zia o _ nor, di Scozia o_
soar In peace and war, May Ban - quo's fame for-ev - er

ALL°. AGITATO ♩ = 144
L
nor.
war!
D
nor, di Scozia o - nor.
soar in peace and war!
M.
nor, di Scozia o - nor.
soar in peace and war!
MACB.
(terrified)
(The ghost reappears.)
Va! Spir_to d'a_bis _ so! Spa_
Go! Hell shall de-stroy you! The
nor, di Scozia o - nor.
soar in peace and war!
nor, di Scozia o - nor.
soar in peace and war!
nor, di Scozia o - nor.
soar in peace and war!
ALL°. AGITATO ♩ = 144
ff
MACB.
lanca u_na fos _ sa, o ter _ ra, l'in_go _ ia.
earth shall rip o - pen and hide you for-ev - -er!

161

DAMA
Sven - tu - ra! ter - ror!
Di - sas - ter and doom!
MACDUFF
Sven - tu - ra! ter - ror!
Di - sas - ter and doom!
M
cor! Quan -
heart! I
Sven - tu - ra! ter - ror!
Di - sas - ter and doom!
Sven - tu - ra! ter - ror!
Di - sas - ter and doom!
Sven - tu - ra! ter - ror!
Di - sas - ter and doom!
27
t'al - tri io pur o - so! di - ven - - - - ta pur
ask you to dare me: A li - - - - on or
ti - - gre, le - on mi - naccio - - so. m'ab -
ti - - ger, you nev - - - - er will scare me. Em -

bran - ca.... Mac - bet - - - to tre - mar non ve -
brace me and see that Mac-beth will not

dra - - i, co - noscer, cono - scer po - trai s'io pro - vi ter -
trem - ble! Or bet-ter, be hu - man a - gain and fight with a

ror! Ma fug - gi! deh, fuggi, fuggi, fuggi, fantasma tre -
sword! But, de - mon, go from me! Leave me! Leave me, you shad-ow, you

(The ghost disappears.)

men - do!
mon - ster!

La vi_ta ri_pren_do!
I'm breath_ing more free_ly.

allarg. a poco a poco

LADY (under her breath, to Macbeth)
DAMA
(Ver_go_gna, si_gnor!)
How shame_ful, my lord! *pp*

MACDUFF
Sven_tu_ra! sven_
pp Di_sas_ter! Di_

Sven_tu_ra! sven_
Di_sas_ter! Di_

pp

Sven_tu_ra! sven_
pp Di_sas_ter! Di_

Sven_tu_ra! sven_
pp Di_sas_ter! Di_

Sven_tu_ra! sven_
Di_sas_ter! Di_

pp

46438

tu - ra! / sas - ter!

MACBETH LARGO ♩ = 50 *sotto voce*

San - gue a me, quell'om - bra
'Twill have blood, this ghost - ly

166

chie—de, e l'a-vrà, l'avrà, lo
de———mon, and I swear, I swear, 'twill

giu_ro! Il ve-la_me,il vela_me del fu-
have___it! Let the witch—es who can di-vine to-

tu_ro alle stre_ghe, alle stre-ghe squarcierò, alle streghe squarcie-
mor-row, tell my fu-ture, bare my fate, tear-ing a cur-tain that no one else can

con forza

167

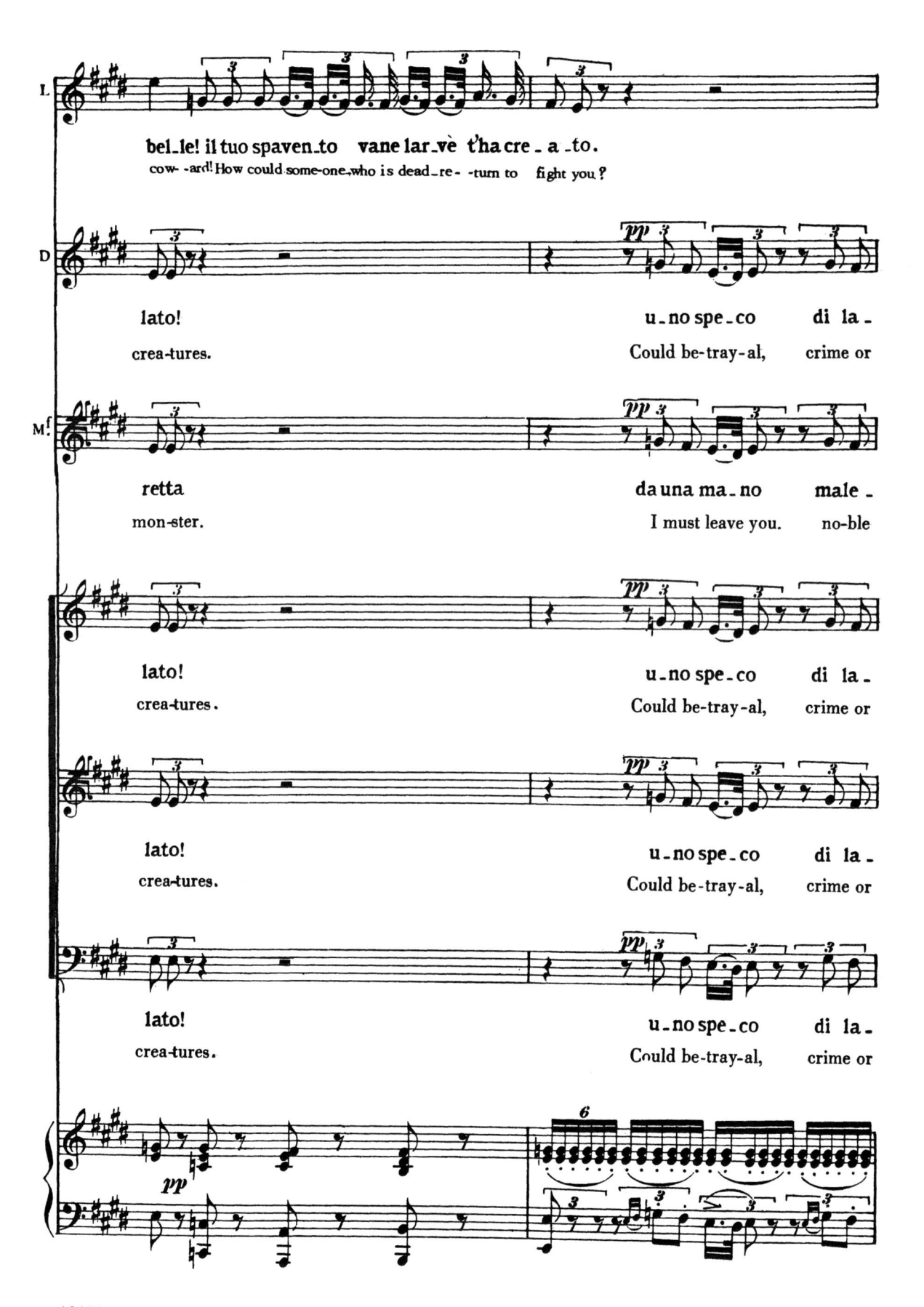

bel-le! il tuo spaven-to vane lar-ve t'ha cre-a-to.
cow--ard! How could some-one who is dead re--turn to fight you?

lato! u-no spe-co di la-
crea-tures. Could be-tray-al, crime or

retta da una ma-no male-
mon-ster. I must leave you. no-ble

lato! u-no spe-co di la-
crea-tures. Could be-tray-al, crime or

lato! u-no spe-co di la-
crea-tures. Could be-tray-al, crime or

lato! u-no spe-co di la-
crea-tures. Could be-tray-al, crime or

169

Il de-lit-to è consuma-to, chi morì tor-nar non
What is done, don't let it smite you with— ter-ror and—

dro-ni questa ter-ra di-ven-tò,
mur-der run a-foul of right and law?

det-ta vi-ver so-lo il reo vi può.
coun-try, doomed to ter-ror no one fore-saw.

dro-ni questa ter-ra di-ven-tò,
mur-der run a-foul of right and law?

dro-ni questa ter-ra di-ven-tò,
mur-der run a-foul of right and law?

dro-ni questa ter-ra di-ven-tò,
mur-der run a-foul of right and law?

L: può, il de_lit_to è consu_mato, è con_su-
awe! What is done,___ is done_and_o-ver, is gone and for-

D: diventò, diven_tò,
Of the law? Of the law?

M: Bie__chi ar_ca_ni! s'ab_ban_doni
Fear_____ and hor-ror cast__ their shad-ow

MACBETH: San__gue a_me quell'ombra chiede,
Blood_____ it asks_for, this_ghost-ly de-mon,

diventò, diven_tò,
Of the law? Of the law?

diventò, diventò,
Of the law? Of the law?

171

172

173

L
D
M.f
M
f
cresc.
può, chi morì, chi mo - rì tornar non può, no, tornar, no, non
awe! Who is dead can-not fight and shall not smite you with ter-ror and
tò, diventò, di - ven - tò, ah, que - sta ter - ra, ah, sì, di - ven -
law? Could a crime or a mur - der be a men-ace to jus-tice and
può, viver sol, vi - ver sol il reo vi può, solo il re - o vi
saw. To a fate, to a reign of death and ter-ror that no one fore -
vrà, e l'avrà e l'a - vrà, l'avrà, lo giuro, lo giuro, l'a -
have. This I swear, this I swear, I swear that blood it will have, This I
diventò diventò, que - sta terra diventò, diven -
Of the law. of the law? How could it threat - en the law, what he
diventò diventò, que - sta terra diventò, diven -
Of the law. of the law? How could it threat - en the law, what he
diventò diventò, que - sta terra diventò, diven -
Of the law, of the law? How could it threat - en the law, what he

175

176

177

178

ma - to, il de-litto è con-su-
got - ten, What is done must be for-

tò, di - - ven-
law? Of the

può, vi
I shall

ro, il ve-la-me del fu-tu - - - -
row, Let the witch-es tell my fu - - - -

tò, di - - ven-
law? Of the

di - - ven-
Of the

tò, di - - ven-
law? Of the

46438

179

180

L: nar,— tornar— non può,— tor-nar— non
rise— no more.— will rise— no more. So

D: tò, que-sta ter - ra di ven
tray - al or mur - der be a

M: può,— vi - ver so - lo il re - o vi
land,— I shall leave— this coun - try of

M: al - le stre - ghe
from their se - crets,

tò, sì, di ven -
crime be - come a

tò, sì, di ven -
crime be - come a

tò, sì, di ven -
crime be - come a

46438

181

può. / awe?
tò. Biechi arca_ni! sgomen_ta_to da fan_ta_smi egli ha par_
law? Fear and hor-ror mark his fea-tures, While he curs-es un-ho-ly

può. Biechi arca_ni! s'abban_do_ni que_sta ter_ra; or ch'ella è
saw. Fear and hor-ror cast their shad-ow On a fu-ture ruled by a

rò. / draw.
tò. Biechi arca_ni! sgomen_ta_to da fan_ta_smi egli ha par_
law? Fear and hor-ror mark his fea-tures, While he curs-es un-ho-ly

tò. Biechi arca_ni! sgomen_ta_to da fan_ta_smi egli ha par_
law? Fear and hor-ror mark his fea-tures, While he curs-es un-ho-ly

tò. Biechi arca_ni! sgomen_ta_to da fan_ta_smi egli ha par_
law? Fear and hor-ror mark his fea-tures, While he curs-es un-ho-ly

tornar, tornar non può, tornar, tornar non può,
Why stand in fear and awe? Why stand in fear and awe?

la — to! u — no spe — co di la —
crea — tures. Could be- tray — al, crime or

ret — ta da u — na ma — no ma — le —
mon — ster. I must leave — you, no — ble

l'avrà, l'avrà, lo giu — ro, l'avrà, l'avrà, lo giu — ro,
I swear that it will have it! I swear that it will have it!

la — to! u — no spe — co di la —
crea — tures. Could be- tray — al, crime or

la — to! u — no spe — co di la —
crea — tures. Could be- tray — al, crime or

la — to! u — no spe — co di la —
crea — tures. Could be- tray — al, crime or

L
non può, non può, il delitto è consu -
In fear and awe? What is done must be for -
D
droni questa ter-ra di - ven-tò, di - - ven -
mur-der run a - foul of right and law? Of the
Mf
det-ta vi-ver so-lo il reo vi può, vi
coun-try, doomed to ter-ror no one fore-saw, Yes,
M
e l'avrà, lo-giu - ro, il velame del fu-tu - - - -
This I swear, I swear it! Let the ones who know tomor - - - - -
droni questa ter-ra di - ven-tò, di - - ven -
mur-der run a - foul of right - and law? Of the
droni questa ter-ra di - ven-tò,
mur-der run a - foul of right - and law?
droni questa ter-ra di - ven-tò, di - - ven -
mur-der run a - foul of right and law? Of the

ma - to, il de - litto è con - su -
got - - ten! What is done must be for -

tò, di - - - ven -
law? Of the

può, vi
I shall

ro, il ve - la - me del fu - tu - - - -
row, Let the witch-es tell my fu - - - -

tò, di - - - ven -
law? Of the

di - - - ven -
Of the

tò, di - - - ven -
law? Of the

186

ma - to, chi mo - rì — tor -
got - ten, and the dead — will

tò, di — — — ven -
law? Can be -

può, vi
leave this

ro al - le stre - ghe squarcie - rò,
ture, Yes, the cur - tain they will draw

tò, di — — — ven -
law? Can a

tò, di — — — ven -
law? Can a

tò, di — — — ven -
law? Can a

46438

187

188

189

190

può, chi morì tornar non può, tornar non
awe? Since the dead can-not re-turn, why stand in

tò, divento, ah questa terra diven-
law? Can a crime, shame-ful and vile, threat-en the

può, sol vi può, ah viver sol il reo vi
saw. Ah, de-spair, ter-ror and death no one fore-

rò, alle streghe squarcierò, io squarcie-
draw! Yes, the veil they shall with-draw, they shall with-

divento,
For the law!

questa terra divento, divento,
Let us pray for the law, for the law!

questa terra divento, divento,
Let us pray for the law, for the law!

[32]

46438

191

End of Act II

ACT III

A Dark Cave

In the center a boiling cauldron surrounded by witches, thunder and lightning.

193

Sop. 3. *pp*
Tre vol_te miagola la gatta in fre — — go_la.
Three times yam-mer-ing a rov-ing cat I heard.

Sop. 2. *pp*
Tre vol_te l'upupa lamenta ed u — — lu_la.
Three times stammering the sleeping boar has stirred.

Sop. 1. *pp*
Tre vol_te l'istri_ce gua_i_sce al ven — — —
Three times clam-or-ing the owl has hoot —

Sop. 1.
to. Questo è il mo_men_to. Su via! sol_leci_te
ed. All is well suit-ed! The pot fill bus-i-ly,

Sop. 2.
Questo è il mo_men_to. Su via! sol_leci_te
All is well suit-ed! The pot fill bus-i-ly,

Sop. 3.
Questo è il mo_men_to. Su via! sol_leci_te
All is well suit-ed! The pot fill bus-i-ly,

giriam la pento_la, mesciamvi in circolo pos_
And stir it diz-zi-ly, till wile and witch-er-y a-

giriam la pento_la, mesciamvi in circolo pos_
And stir it diz-zi-ly, till wile and witch-er-y a-

giriam la pento_la, mesciamvi in circolo pos_
And stir it diz-zi-ly, till wile and witch-er-y a-

sen_ti in_tin_go_li;
new will brew our witch-es' stew.

sen_ti in_tin_go_li;
new will brew our witch-es' stew.

sen_ti in_tin_go_li;
new will brew our witch-es' stew.

si - roc-chie, al-l'o-pra, all'o-pra, al-
Come, gath-er round! Be-ware what
si - roc-chie, al-l'o-pra, all'o-pra, al-
Come, gath-er round! Be-ware what
si - roc-chie, al-l'o-pra, all'o-pra, al-
Come, gath-er round! Be-ware what
3
f
l'o-pra, all'o - - pra! l'ac-qua già fu-ma, fu - -
each is do - - ing! Be-hold the caul-dron spew - -
l'o-pra, all'o - - pra! l'ac-qua già fu-ma, fu - -
each is do - - ing! Be-hold the caul-dron spew - -
l'o-pra, all'o - - pra! l'ac-qua già fu-ma, fu - -
each is do - - ing! Be-hold the caul-dron spew - -
ff

197

go - glia nel va - so in - fer - nal, va, cuo - ci e gor -
tum - ble, and writhe and squirm and swell, While o - ver you we

go - glia nel va - so infer - nal.
mum - ble the an-cient witches' spell!

Sop. 2.ⁱ (likewise)
Tu, lin - gua di vi - pera, tu, pelo di not - to - la, tu,
An eye - lid, a vi - per's jaw, the tip of a how-let's wing! Some

S.ⁱ 2.ⁱ
san - gue di sci - mia, tu, dente di bot - to - lo, va, bol - li e t'av -
bat - blood, a ti - ger claw, the hook on a spi - der's sting! Now fuse and ooze and
S.ⁱ 2.ⁱ
vol - to - la nel bro - do in - fer - nal, va, bol - li e t'av -
lose your scent, And scald and seethe and smell, Till, tast - ing sweet and
pp
S.ⁱ 2.ⁱ
vol - tola nel bro - do infer - nal.
suc - cu-lent, The witch - es' brew will jell!
8
ff
pp

Sop. I. (likewise)

Tu, di- to d'un par- golo stroz- zato nel na- sce- re, tu,
The thumb of an or-phan-child, Killed off in a lone-ly trench! The

lab- bro d'un Tar- taro, tu, cor d'un e- re- ti- co, va
nose of a Tar- tar wild, The heart of a hea- then wench! Now

den- tro, e con- so- li- da la pol- ta in- fer- nal,— va
burn and turn more sa- vor- y, un- til we all can tell— The

den- tro, e con- so- li- da la pol- ta in- fer- nal.
strong and spic- y fla- vor of the dain- ty broth of Hell!

201

202

me - scere ben sa - pe - te, rime - sce - te! ri - me - scete!
those who han-dle it flaw-less-ly Are per-mit-ted to han-dle the mat-ter.

me - scere ben sa - pe - te, rime - sce - te! ri - me - scete!
those who han-dle it flaw-less-ly Are per-mit-ted to han-dle the mat-ter.

me - scere ben sa - pe - te, rime - sce - te! ri - me - scete!
those who han-dle- it flaw-less-ly Are per-mit-ted to han-dle the mat-ter.

E voi, spir-ti negri e can-didi, rime-sce-te, ri - me-
Wick-ed witch-es, gob-lins, all of you, Bet-ter come and stir the

E voi, spir-ti negri e can-didi, rime-sce-te, ri - me-
Wick-ed witch-es, gob-lins, all of you, Bet-ter come and stir the

E voi, spir-ti negri e can-didi, rime-sce-te, ri - me-
Wick-ed witch-es, gob-lins, all of you, Bet-ter come and stir the

46438

204

sce_te, voi che mescere ben sa_pe_te, ri_me_sce_te, ri me_
work to do, when witch-es pre-pare the bat-ter! Let us taste, not waste, the

sce_te, voi che me_scere ben sa_pe_te, voi che me_scer ben sa_
dain_ty stew, The won-der-ful witch - es' brew! From far and wide through filth-y

ff p ff p
pe - te, che me - scer ben sa - pe - te, che me - scer ben sa -
air — Did we witch - es come to share — in this most mo - men - tous
pe - te, che me - scer ben sa - pe - te, che me - scer ben sa -
air — Did we witch - es come to share — in this most mo - men - tous
pe - te, che me - scer ben sa - pe - te, che me - scer ben sa -
air — Did we witch - es come to share — in this most mo - men - tous
incalz. sempre
pe - te, ri - me - sce - te, ri - me - sce - te, ri - me - sce - - -
mat - ter. Mis - be - got - ten, foul and rot - ten, work and wor - - -
pe - te, ri - me - sce - te, ri - me - sce - te, ri - me - sce - - -
mat - ter. Mis - be - got - ten, foul and rot - ten, work and wor - - -
pe - te, ri - me - sce - te, ri - me - sce - te, ri - me - sce - - -
mat - ter. Mis - be - got - ten, foul and rot - ten, work and wor - - -
8
incalz. sempre

207

BALLET

(The stage comes alive with spirits, devils, goblins, etc., all dancing around the cauldron.)

209

210

(The dance stops as the dancers invoke Hecate, the goddess of night and witchcraft.)

212

(Hecate appears.)

(Everyone remains motionless while looking at the goddess.)

14 (Hecate expresses to the witches her awareness of their work and of the reasons why she had been summoned.)

(Hecate surveys everything with care.)

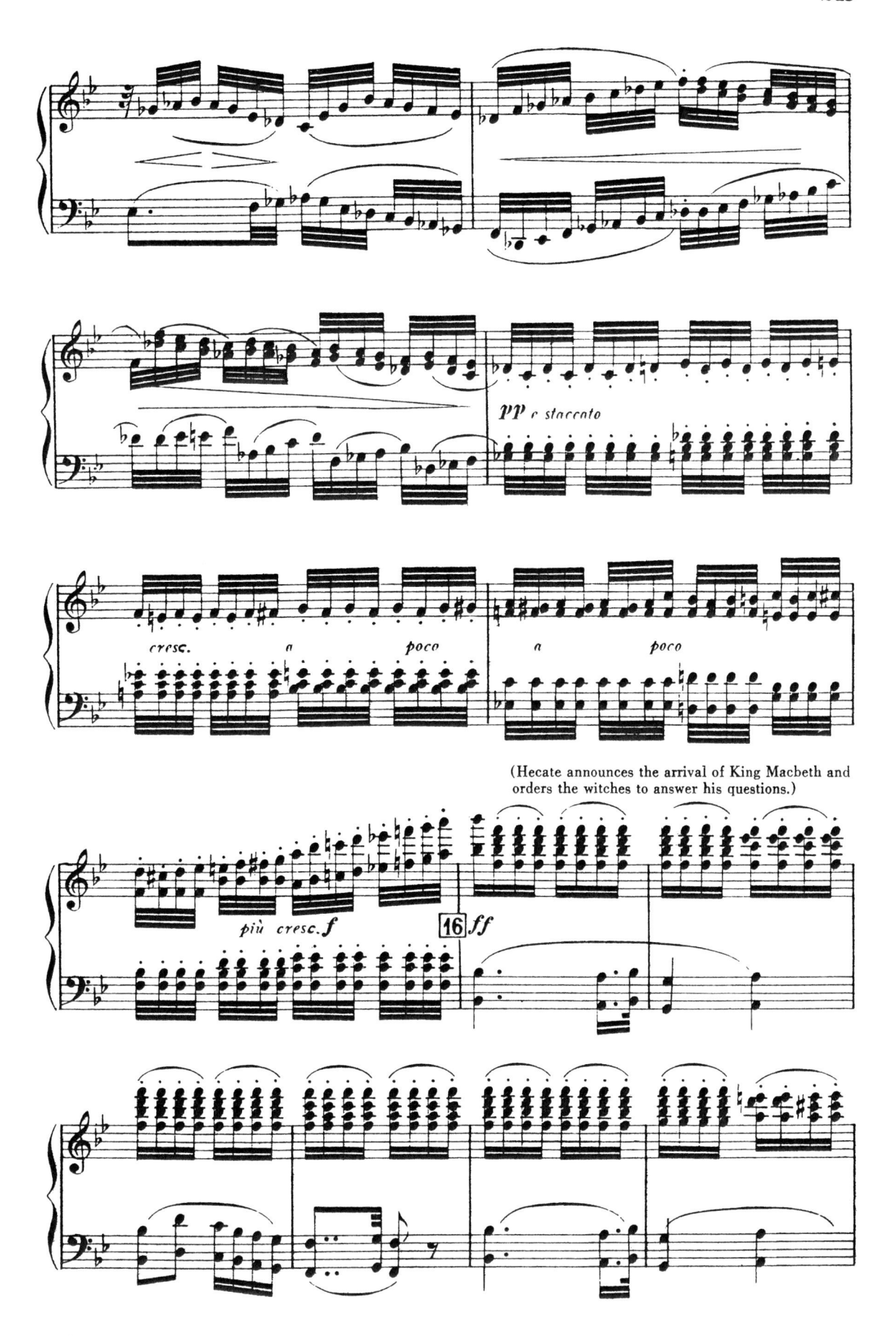

(Hecate announces the arrival of King Macbeth and orders the witches to answer his questions.)

216

(Should Macbeth's composure break down, the spirits of the air are to revive and reinvigorate him.)

cresc.

sempre più cresc.

(But Macbeth's destruction shall not be delayed any longer.)

46438

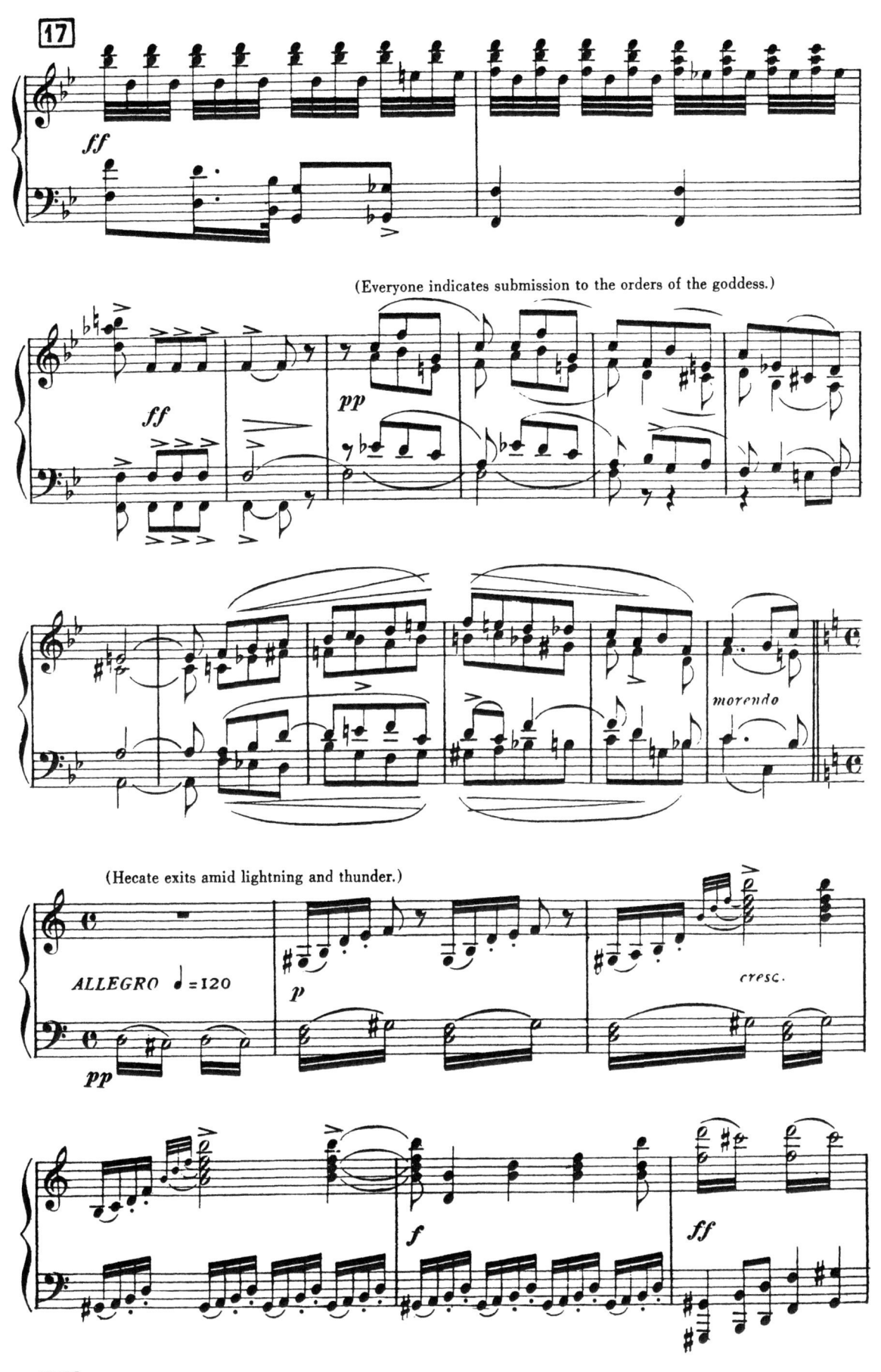

(Everyone indicates submission to the orders of the goddess.)

morendo

(Hecate exits amid lightning and thunder.)

ALLEGRO ♩ = 120

Waltz

ALL^o. VIVACISSIMO ♩. = 84

219

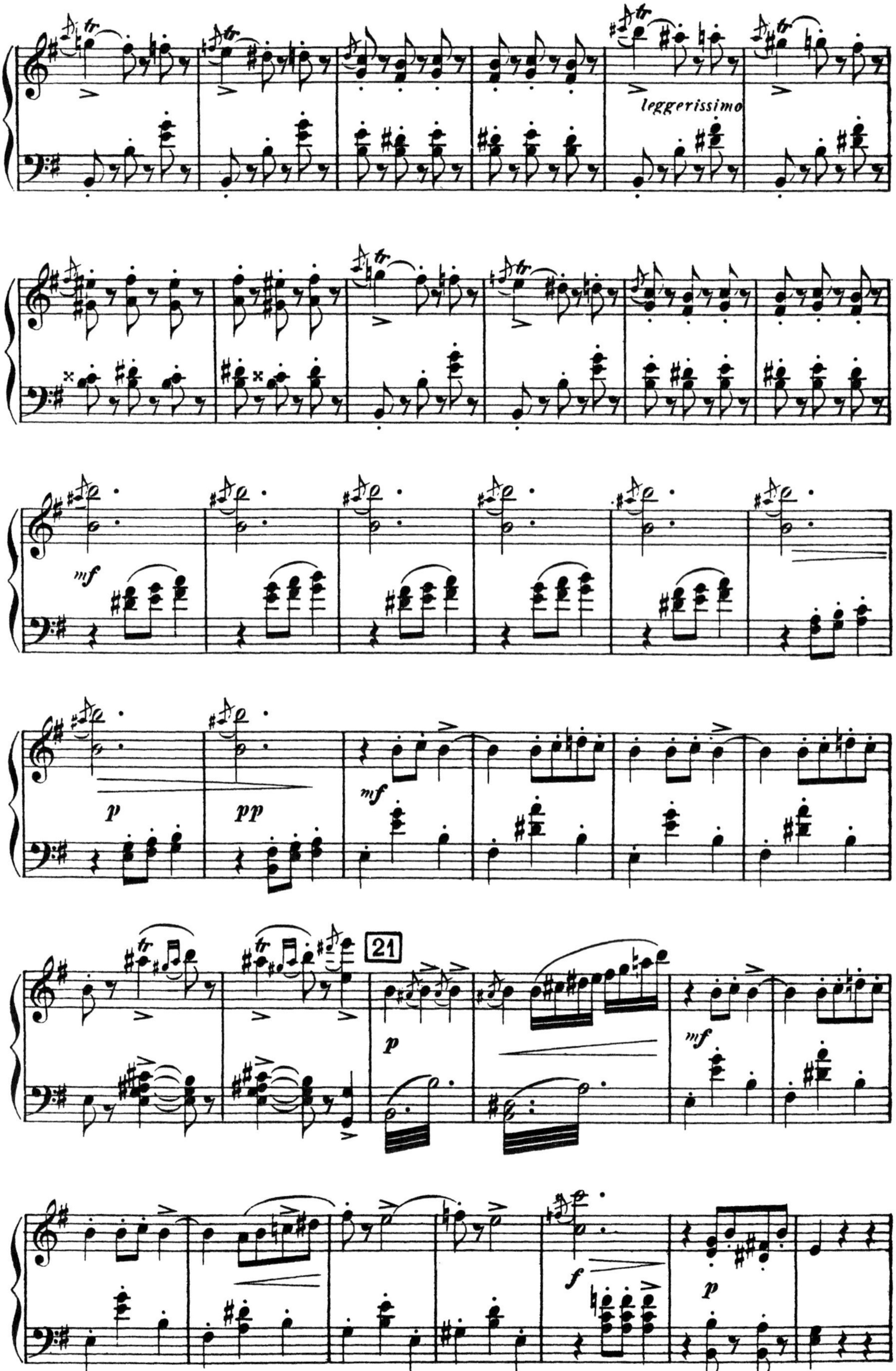
leggerissimo
mf
p
pp
21
f

221

(They all form a wide circle and, holding hands, dance around the cauldron.)

24 POCO PIÙ MOSSO ♩. = 96

223

ALLEGRO ♩. = 88
pp
MACBETH (entering, to some of his men)
Finchè ap_pelli, si_lenti m'atten_de_te.
Stay in si-lence and wait un-til I call you!
ALL.° MOD.to ♩ = 80
f
(advancing towards the witches)
Che fa_te voi, mi_ste_rï_o_se donne?
What is't you do, you se-cret, night-ly crea-tures?
Per que.
I con -
(solemnly)
Sop. I.i
Sop. 2.i
Sop. 3.i
CORO DI STREGHE.
U_n'o_pra sen_za nome.
A deed with-out a name.

st'opra infernal io vi scongiuro! ch'io sappia il mio destin, se cielo e
jure you by all your eerie powers: Reply to what I ask! And if by

terra dovessero innovar l'antica guerra!
telling You should destroy the world, I want your answer.

CORO DI STREGHE
Dalle incognite posse udir lo vuoi, cui ministre obbediam, oppur da noi?
Would you rather receive it from us, who do what our Demons command, or from our masters?

POCO PIÙ LENTO ♩ = 69

MAC.
Evocatele pur, se del futuro mi possono chiarir l'enigma oscuro.
Call upon them at once! Let them inform me, Reveal the secret fate that lies before me!

46438

26 ANDte MAESTOSO ♩ = 66
ff
CORO DI STREGHE
Dal_le basse e dall'al_te re_gio - ni,
From the deep, from on high, from on yon - der,
spirti er_
Ghost-ly
ran_ti, sa_li _ te, scen _ de - te!
de-mons, we bid you as - sem - ble!
(Preceded by a lightning bolt, a man's head appears, wearing a helmet.)
27
MAC.
Dimmi, o spir - to...
I en - treat you...
T'ha letto nel
He fath-oms your

co - re; taci e n'o - di le vo - ci se - grete.
rea - son. Do not ask him and lis - ten in - si - lence!

APPARIZIONE
O Mac - bet - to! Macbet - to! Mac -
Mac - beth! — Mac-beth! Mac -

MAC.
bet - to! da Mac - duf - fo ti guar - da pru - den - te.
beth! — Beware Mac - duff! — Beware the Thane of Fife!

Tu m'afforzi l'accolto so -
You con-firm — my fear and sus -

(to the apparition) (The head vanishes.)
M
spetto! Solo un motto....
pi - cion. Let me ask you...

CORO
Richie - ste non vuo - - le. Ecco un al - tro di lui più pos -
He will not be com-mand - ed. Here's an - oth - er, more po-tent than the

(Thunder accompanies the appearance of a bloody child.)
sen - te.
first one!
ff
p
Ta-ci,e n'o-di l'occul-te pa-ro-le.
Do not speak! Try to grasp what he tells you!
APPARIZIONE
Soprano
O Mac - bet-to! Macbet-to! Mac-
Mac - beth! - Mac-beth! - Mac-
fp
A
bet - to! Es - ser puoi sangui-na-rio, fe - ro - ce: nes-sun na-to di don-na ti
beth! - Nei-ther blood-shed nor doubt shall a-larm you. No one born of a wom-an can
A
(disappears)
nuo - ce.
harm you.
MAC.
cantando, con espansione
O Macduf-fo, tua vi-ta per-
Live, Mac-duff, for I fear you no
ff
p

ALL°. 𝅗𝅥 = 100 cambiando istantaneamente
(wildly)
M
do_no, tua vi_ta per - dono! No! no! no! no! mor_
long-er, I fear you no long-er! No, no, no, no! You will
29
f
ALL°. 𝅗𝅥 = 100
pp staccato
rai! Sul re_ga - - le mio pet_to doppio u_sber - go_sa -
die! Like a shield dou-bly plat-ed, that will cov - er_my_
cresc.
rà,___ doppio u_sber_go sa_rà la tua morte!
heart,___ so your death shall grant me two- -fold pro_tec-tion.
6
f
ff
(Thunder and lightning. A child appears, wearing a crown and holding a little tree.)
ff

AND.te SOSTENUTO ♩ = 66
MAC.
ppp parlante
voce muta
sempre più p
Ma che av-visa quel lampo, quel tuono? Un fan-
What is fore-cast by light-ning and thun-der? 'Tis a
AND.te SOSTENUTO ♩ = 66
pp
f
M
ciullo col serto dei re!
child, yet crowned like a king.
APPARIZIONE
Sop.
Sta d'a-ni-mo
Be proud and cou-
CORO
ppp
Taci, ed o-di!
Hark in si-lence!
dim.
morendo
fp
A
for-te: glo-rï-o-so, invin-ci-bil sa-rai fin che il bo-sco di Bir-na ve-
ra-geous! Bright and high stands your star in the skies, Till the for-est of Bir-nam shall
fp
MAC.
Oh! lieto au-
30
(disappears) Oh! joy-ous
A
drai rav-vï-ar-si e ve-nir con-tro te!
rise, And at last shall ad-vance up-on you.
fp
ff
6
6.

ALLEGRO 𝅗𝅥 = 100
M
gu - rio! oh lie - to au - gurio! Per ma - gica pos - sa, per
tid - ings, oh wel - come pre - dic - tion! No pow'r ev - er grant - ed, sub -
pp
ALLEGRO 𝅗𝅥 = 100
pp
ma - gica possa sel - va al - cu - na giammai non fu mos - -
lime or en - chant - ed, Can by charm move a tree firm - ly plant - -
sa, no, giamma - i non fu mos - - - - - sa, no, sel - va al -
ed, Can up - root a might - y for - - - - - est. No spell can
cu - na non fu mossa, giam - mai, no, giammai! Or mi
bid a for - est rise, cause a for - est to rise. De - mons,
(to the witches)
p

M: dite: sa - li - re al mio soglio la pro-ge-nie di Ban-co do-vrà?
tell me: The chil - dren of Ban-quo... Will they one day be wear-ing my crown?

CORO: Lo voglio! lo voglio! o su voi la mia spada ca-drà!
Your an-swer! Your an-swer! Or at once shall my sword strike you down!

Non cer-carlo!
Do not ask us!

(The cauldron sinks into the ground.)

M: La cal-
Now the

233

da_ ia è spa_ ri_ta!   per_chè?
caul-dron has van-ished.   But why?

ADAGIO ♩ = 68

32   Qual con_cento!   Parla_te! che
Strains un_ho-ly!   But what do they

(The sound of bagpipes is heard underground.)

v'è?
mean?

Sop. 1:

Ap_pa_ri_te!
Show and grieve him!

Sop. 2:

Ap_pa_ri_te!
Show and grieve him!

Sop. 3:

Ap_pa_ri_te!
Show and grieve him!

46438

234

235

236

un ter-zo?
A third one...

(Another king.) (Another king.)
un quar-to?
a fourth one...

un quin-to?
a fifth one!

(The sixth king.)

(The eighth king is Banquo, holding a mirror.)

MAC.
Oh! mio terror! del-
And yet one more! A

(The seventh.)

238

(Drawing his sword, Banquo attacks the apparitions.)
M
di - ta! Muo - ri, fatal pro - ge - nie!
strong - er! Un - ho - ly breed, I'll kill you....
f
(He recoils.)
p
Ah! che non hai tu vi - ta! ahi vi - sta! ahi
You are a - live no long - er. Oh ter - ror! Oh
p
vi - sta! ah! ah! che non hai tu vi - ta, non hai tu
ter - ror! Ah! You are a - live no long - er, a - live no
ff
35
ff
vi - ta, non hai, non hai tu vi - ta! ahi vi - sta! ahi
long - er. You are a - live no long - er! Oh ter - ror! Oh
p

240

Ballet with Chorus

(The spirits of the air descend gradually.)

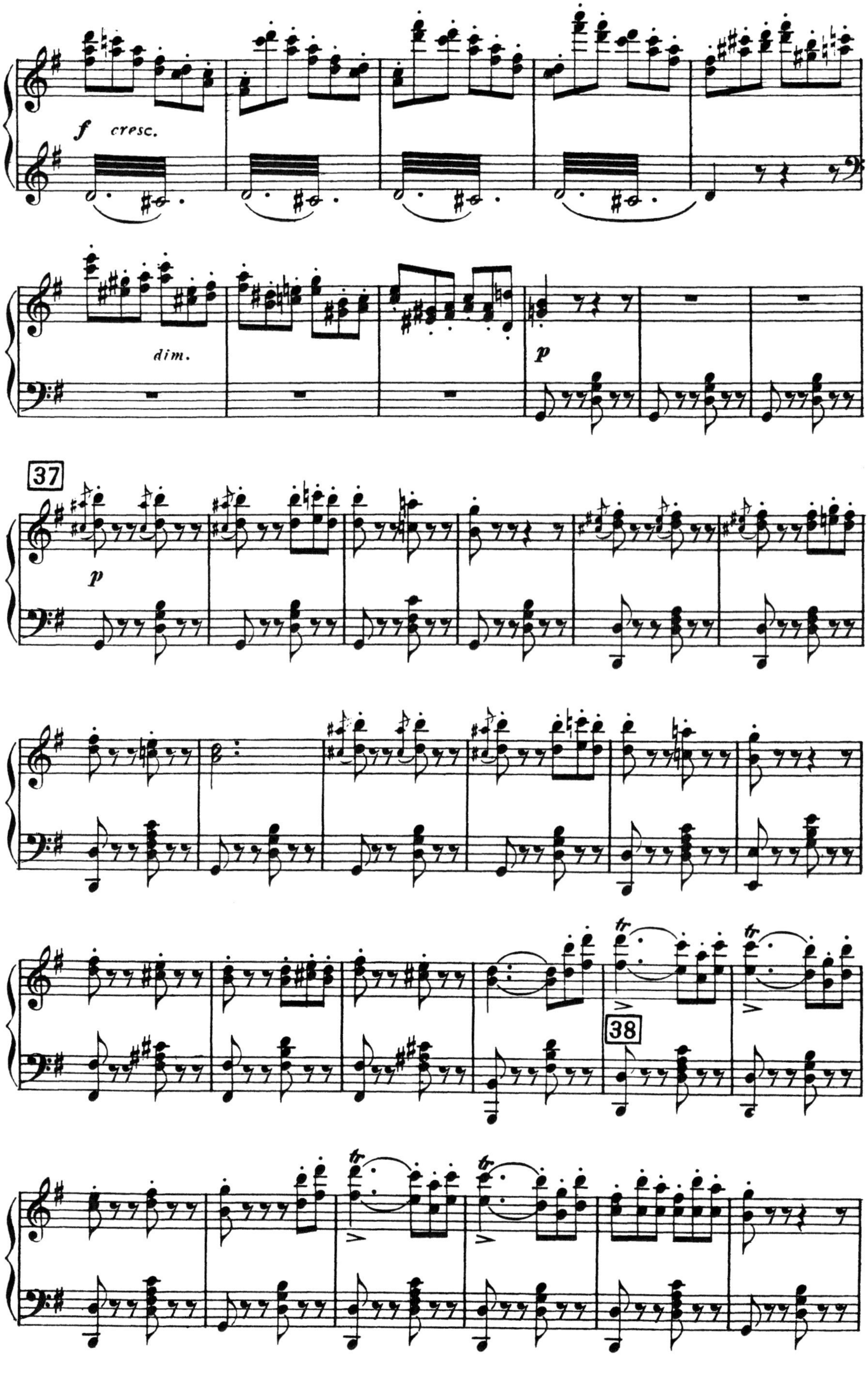
f cresc.
dim.
p
37
p
tr
38

CORO DI STREGHE
tutto sotto voce e staccato
On - dine e sil - fidi, dal - l'a - li candide, su quella pal - li - da
Elves of the night, fly to the ground and bring to him Cool, ten-der com-fort your
p
fron - te spi - ra - te. Tes - sete in vor - tice ca - ro - le ar - mo - niche,
wings have to of - fer! Lilt - ing and light, gath-er a-round and sing to him,
e sensi ed a - nima gli con - for - tate, e — sen - si ed — a - nima
Eas - ing the tor - ment his mind must suf-fer, Re - liev - ing the — ag - o-ny
tr
39
gli confor - tate, e — sen - si ed — a - nima gli confor - tate.
he has to suf-fer! Re - liev - ing the - ag - o-ny he has to suf-fer!
tr

244

(The spirits dance.)

p leggermente

CORO

E sen - si ed a - nima
Re - liev-ing the ag - o-ny

gli confor-tate, e sen - si ed a - nima gli confor-tate.
he has to suf-fer! Re - liev-ing the ag - o-ny he has to suf-fer!

pp

46438

CORO

Ondine e silfidi, dall'ali candide, su quella pallida fronte spirate. Tes se te in vortice ca-
Elves of the night, fly to the ground and bring to him Cool, tender comfort your wings have to offer! Lilt- ing and light, gath-er a-

ro - le ar - mo - niche e sensi ed a - nima gli con - for -
round and sing to him, Eas - ing the tor - ment his mind must

tate, e sen - si ed a - nima gli con - for - tate, e
suf-fer, Re - liev - ing the ag - o - ny he has to suf-fer! Re -

sen - si ed a - ni - ma gli con - for - ta - te, e
liev - ing the ag - o - ny he has to suf - fer!

247

248

gli confor - ta — — — — te.
you shall re - lieve — — — — him!

FINALE 3

M
LADY
co - ra le streghe inter-ro-gai! E dis-ser?
witch - es I came to ask once more. Their an-swer?
ppp
MAC.
sotto voce (with an air of mystery)
Da Mac-duff ti guarda!
'Be- ware Mac-duff!'—
LADY
Segui...
Fur-ther!
MAC.
sempre sotto voce
Te non uc-ci-de-
'You shall not die' by the
LADY
Se-gui...
Fur-ther!
M
rà na-to di don-na.
hand of one born of wom-an.'
Invit-to sa-rai finchè la sel-va di
'Your glo-ry will last un-til the for-est of
M
Bir-na contro te non mo-va.
Bir-nam shall a-rise a-gainst you.'
LADY
Se-gui...
Fur-ther!
MAC.
with full voice
Ma pur di
Yet, I saw

252

sangue si sperda a noi nemico!
blood flow like water, spilled in this slaughter!

LADY *con espansione*
Or riconosco il tuo coraggio antico!
Ah, at last I hear again the valiant man I ad-

46 *ff*

ALL⁰. ASSAI ♩=160

ti-co! Tuo-na, rimp-
mire! O-pen, o
O-ra di morte e di vendetta,
Rise, day of doom, bloody dawn of destruction!

bomba per l'orbe intero
womb of disaster and terror!
come assordante l'atro pen-
Drown in your thunder my gloom and de-

del cor le fi - bre tutte intro - nò!
Come, rend a - sun - der the qualms of the heart!

sie - ro o - ra di
jec - tion! Dawn of de-

e di ven - det - ta, ven
Mur - - - der and venge - ance! ...of

mor - te ven-
struc - tion, of

detta, ven - detta, ven - det - ta,
mur-der, de - struc-tion and venge - ance!

(sliding down)

detta, ven - detta, ven - det - ta,
mur-der, de - struc-tion, and venge - ance!

255

POCO RITENUTO
pppp

o — ra di mor — te o — mai, omai t'af —
Come, dawn of doom, a — rise in blood and

pppp subdued, but with greatest intensity

o — ra di mor — te o — mai, omai t'af —
Come, dawn of doom, a — rise in blood and

fret — ta! In — can — cel — la — bi — le il
ter — ror! Drawn by our des — ti — ny, we

fret — ta! In — can — cel — la — bi — le il
ter — ror! Drawn by our des — ti — ny, we

fa — to ha scritto, il fato ha scritto, il fato ha
do what is writ-ten, do what is writ-ten, do what is

fa — to ha scritto, il fato ha scritto, il fato ha
do what is writ-ten, do what is writ-ten, do what is

46438

portando la voce
A tempo agitato
come prima
ff
L
scrit - - - - to: de - ve il de -
writ - - - - ten. Let it be
portando la voce
ff
M
scrit - - - - to: l'im - pre-sa compier
writ - - - - ten. Let it be end-ed
48
A tempo agitato
come prima
p
p
cresc.
lit - to, poi - chè col san - - gue col
end - ed in blood and ter - - - ror, In
cresc.
de - ve de - ve il delit - - to, poichè col
in blood, in blood and in ter - - ror! Ah, let in
cresc.
ff
san - - - gue s'i - nau - gu - rò, poi - chè col sangue s'inaugu -
slaugh - - - ter now end the fate - ful deed, The deed that was born of
ff
san - - - gue s'i - nau - gu - rò, poi - chè col sangue s'inaugu -
slaugh - - - ter now end the fate - ful deed, The deed that was born of
ff
dim.
p

257

End of Act III

ACT IV

Scene 1

A deserted spot along the border between Scotland and England.
A Group of Refugees from Scotland

Soprani
Tenori
Bassi
CORO
ppp
Patria op-pressa!
Death and ash-es!
Patria op-
Death and
pressa!
ash-es!
pp
il dol-ce no-me, no, di madre aver non puoi,
Be-lov-ed land, I may no long-er call you home.
p
f

or che tutta a' figli tuoi sei conversa in un avel!
Once a realm of joy and bloom, now a vast and silent tomb!

or che tutta a' figli tuoi sei conversa in un avel!
now a vast and silent tomb!

or che tutta a' figli tuoi sei conversa in un avel!
Once a realm of joy and bloom, now a vast and silent tomb!

Soli Soprani I. *tristissimo*

D'orfanelli e di piangenti chi lo sposo e chi la
Hungry orphans seek their mothers, Sons and daugh-ters mourn their

Sop. I.

prole al venir del nuovo sole s'alza un grido e fere il
fathers. In despair their cries each morning Rise to Heaven's mighty

Sop. 2. e 3.

del nuovo sole s'alza un grido e fere il
their cries each morning Rise to Heaven's mighty

ciel. A quel grido il ciel ri - spon - de quasi voglia impie - to -
dome. And the sky they rend a - sun - der Will re - ply with roaring
ciel. il ciel ri - spon - de im - pie - to -
dome. rend it a - sun - der with roar-ing
Ten. I.
il ciel ri - spon - de im - pie - to -
Ten. 2.
rend it a - sun - der with roar-ing
A quel grido il ciel ri - spon - de quasi voglia impie - to -
Bassi
And the sky they rend a - sun - der Will re - ply with roar-ing
il ciel ri - spon - de im - pie - to -
rend it a - sun - der with roar-ing
si - to propa - gar per l'in - fi - ni - to, Patria op - pres - sa, il tuo do -
thun - der. From on high re-sounds the an - swer: Death and ash - es! Un-hap-py
si - to per l'in - fi - ni - to, Patria op - pres - sa, il tuo do -
thun - der to sound the an - swer: Death and ash - es! Un-hap-py
si - to propa - gar per l'in - fi - ni - to, Patria op - pres - sa, il tuo do -
thun - der. From on high re-sounds the an - swer: Death and ash - es! Un-hap-py
si - to per l'in - fi - ni - to, Patria op - pres - sa, il tuo do -
thun - der to sound the an - swer: Death and ash - es! Un-hap-py
si - to propa - gar per l'in - fi - ni - to, Pa - tria op - pres - sa, il tuo do -
thun - der. From on high re-sounds the an-swer: Death and ash - es! Un-hap-py
3

dolente
pp
lor! Suona a mor - to ognor la
home! Tolls of mourn pp - ing peal out un-
lor! Suona a mor - -
home! Tolls of mourn - -
dolente
pp
lor! Suona a mor - to ognor la
home! Tolls of mourn - ing peal out un-
lor!
home!
pp
lor! Suona a mor - to
home! Tolls of mourn - ing
pp dolente
ppp
pp
squil la, ma nes - su - no audace è tan - to che pur
heed - ed. Awed and haunt - ed by fear and ter - ror No - one
to ognor la squil - la,
ing peal out un-heed - ed.
squil - la, ma nes - su - no audace è tan - to che pur
heed - ed. Awed and haunt - ed by fear and ter - ror No - one
ognor la squil - la, suona a mor - -
peal out un-heed - ed. Tolls of mourn - -

do - ni un va_no pian - to a chi sof _ fre ed a chi
an - swers the call of sor - row. Of com-pas - sion for those who
suona a mor - - to ognor la squil - -
Tolls of mourn - - ing peal out un-heed - -
do - ni un va_no pian - to a chi sof _ fre ed a chi
an - swers the call of sor - row. Of com-pas - sion for those who
to ognor la squil - la,
ing peal out un-heed - ed.
4
muor!_ nessun dona un va_no pian - to a chi soffre ed a chi
die.___ No one dares cry out in sor - row And in grief for those who
la, suona a mor - to, suona a mor -
ed. Tolls of mourn - ing Tolls of mourn -
muor!_ nessun dona un va_no pian - to a chi soffre ed a chi
die.___ No one dares cry out in sor - row And in grief for those who
pp
a chi sof - - fre ed a chi
No one cries for those who
suona a mor - to ognor la squil - - - - - -
Tolls of mourn - - ing peal out un heed - - - - - -
dim.
morendo

264

265

(Enters Macduff.)

MACDUFF — *REC.^{TVO}*

O fi_gli, o fi_gli miei! Da quel ti_ranno tutti ucci_si voi
My chil-dren, my wife and chil-dren! I had to leave you in the fangs of that

ADAGIO

foste, e insiem con vo_i la madre sven_tu_ra_ta!
ti-ger! You were the vic-tims to still his dead-ly fu-ry.

Ah, fra gli ar_ti_gli di quel ti_gre io la_sciai la madre e i fi_gli?
Ah, at the mer-cy of a mon-ster did I leave my wife and chil-dren!

[5] *ADAGIO* ♩ = 50

46438

MACDUFF (sadly)

Ah, la paterna mano non vi fu scudo, o cari, dai perfidi sicari che a morte, a morte vi ferîr! E me fuggiasco, occulto voi chiamavate, voi chiamavate invano col...

Where was, o wife, your husband, Where was, o sons, your father, When in the night would gather The bloody horde to deal you death? Far from my home I languish... In vain you called me in mortal fear and anguish. In

l'ul - ti - mo sin - gul - to, col - l'ul - ti - mo, coll'ultimo re-
vain you whis-pered 'fa - ther', my sons,—— Un-to your last, your dy-ing

spir. Ah! Tram - mi al ti - ranno in fac - cia, Si -
breath. Ah, Lord, when I find the slay - er, my

gno - re, e s'ei mi sfug - ge pos - sa a colui le
sword shall be his ju - ry! Then, should he flee my

brac - cia del tu - o perdo - no a - prir, possa a colui le
fu - ry, may Heav - en for - give Mac - beth! My sword shall be his

braccia, possa a colui le brac — cia del tuo perdono a—
ju — ry, but, should he flee my fu — — ry, May Heav — en for-give Mac-

prir, Si — gnor! pos — sa a colui le braccia del tuo perdono a—
beth. Oh — Lord! Should the ty-rant flee my fu — ry, may God for-give Mac-

(Enters Malcolm leading a host of English soldiers.)

prir.
beth!

7 ALLEGRO ♩ = 80

8
ff
MALCOLM
Do_ve
Where_
Mm
siam? Che bosco è quello?
are we? What wood is this?
Svelga o_
Cut the
CORO
Sop.
La fo_re_sta di Bir_na_mo.
It is called the wood of Bir_nam.
Ten.
La fo_re_sta di Bir_na_mo.
It is called the wood of Bir_nam.
Bassi
La fo_re_sta di Bir_na_mo.
It is called the wood of Bir_nam.
p
p

gnu - no e por - ti un ra - mo, che lo a - scon - da, innan - zi a
for - est! Let our sol - diers be con - cealed by branch and

MACDUFF

Non l'a - vrò, di figli è
Not e - nough! He has no

(to Macduff)
sè! Ti con - for - ti la ven - detta.
tree! Soon you'll slake your thirst for venge-ance.

privo!
children.

Chi non o - dia il suol na - tivo prenda l'armi e se - gua
In our fight for God and coun-try Take up arms and come with

me.
me!

MACD.
ALL°. MAEST.so ♩ = 108
con entusiasmo
La pa - tria tra-di - ta piangen - do ne in - vi - ta! fra - tel - li! gli op-pres-si cor-ria - mo a sal - var!
Our coun - try, we greet you! No crime shall de - feat you! Your hon - or and free - dom no ty - rant shall mar!
MALC. (brandishing their swords)
La pa - tria tra-di - ta piangen - do ne in - vi - ta! fra - tel - li! gli op-pres-si cor-ria - mo a sal - var!
Our coun - try, we greet you! No crime shall de - feat you! Your hon - or and free - dom no ty - rant shall mar!
ALL°. MAEST.so ♩ = 108
Mf.
Mm.
CORO
Sop.
La pa - tria tra-di - ta piangen - do ne in -
Our coun - try, we greet you! No crime shall de -
Ten.
La pa - tria tra - - ta piangen - do ne in -
Our coun - try, we greet you! No crime shall de -
Bassi
La pa - tria tra-di - ta piangen - do ne in -
Our coun - try, we greet you! No crime shall de -

vi - ta! fra-tel - li! gli op-pres - si cor-ria - mo a sal-
feat — you! Your hon - or and free - dom no ty - rant shall

vi - ta! fra-tel - li! gli op-pres - si cor-ria - mo a sal-
feat — you! Your hon - or and free - dom no ty - rant shall

vi - ta! fra-tel - li! gli op-pres - si cor-ria - mo a sal-
feat — you! Your hon - or and free - dom no ty - rant shall

MACD.
Già l'i - ra di - vi - na sul l'em - pio ru -
Our Lord — and Cre - at - or will chas - tise the

MALC.
Già l'i - ra di - vi - na sul l'em - pio ru -
Our Lord — and Cre - at - or will chas - tise the

var!
mar!

var!
mar!

var!
mar!

273

Già l'ira divina sull'empio ru-i-na; gli orribili eccessi l'Eterno stan-
Our Lord and Creator will chastise the traitor, Whose heart knows no mercy, whose fury no

câr,_____ l'E_ter_no stan_ca_ro, l'E_ter_no stan_câr.
bar,_____ Whose pride and am-bi-tion have led__him too far!

câr,_____ l'E_ter_no stan_ca_ro, l'E_ter_no stan_câr.
bar,_____ Whose pride and am-bi-tion have led__him too far!

Gli orri_bili ec_
His heart knows no

Gli orri_bili ec_
His heart knows no

Gli orri_bili ec_
His heart knows no

ces_si l'E_ter_no stancâr,_____ l'E_ter_no stan_ca_ro, l'E_
mer-cy, his fu-ry no bar._____ His pride and am-bi-tion have

ces_si l'E_ter_no stancâr,_____ l'E_ter_no stan_ca_ro, l'E_
mer-cy, his fu-ry no bar._____ His pride and am-bi-tion have

ces_si l'E_ter_no stancâr,_____ l'E_ter_no stan_ca_ro, l'E_
mer-cy, his fu-ry no bar._____ His pride and am-bi-tion have

POCO PIÙ MOSSO ♩ = 160
MACD.
con entusiasmo
Fra - tel - li! gli op - pressi cor - riamo a sal - var! cor -
For free - dom and jus - tice go on - ward to war, Go
MALC.
ter - no
ru - ined him!
11
ff POCO PIÙ MOSSO ♩ = 160
ria - mo, cor - riam, cor - ria - mo, fra - tel - li, gli op - pressi cor -
on - ward in faith and glo - ry! To tum - ble the ty - rant, to
Mf
Mm

lunga
Mf
Mm
riamo a sal_var, cor_ria_ _ mo_ a sal_var, cor_
e_ven the score, U_nit_ _ ed_ in God we are! To
8
lunga
12
riam,_ cor_riam gli op_pressi a sal_var, cor_
e_ven the score go on_ward to war! Go

277

Scene 2

A Hall in Macbeth's Castle.

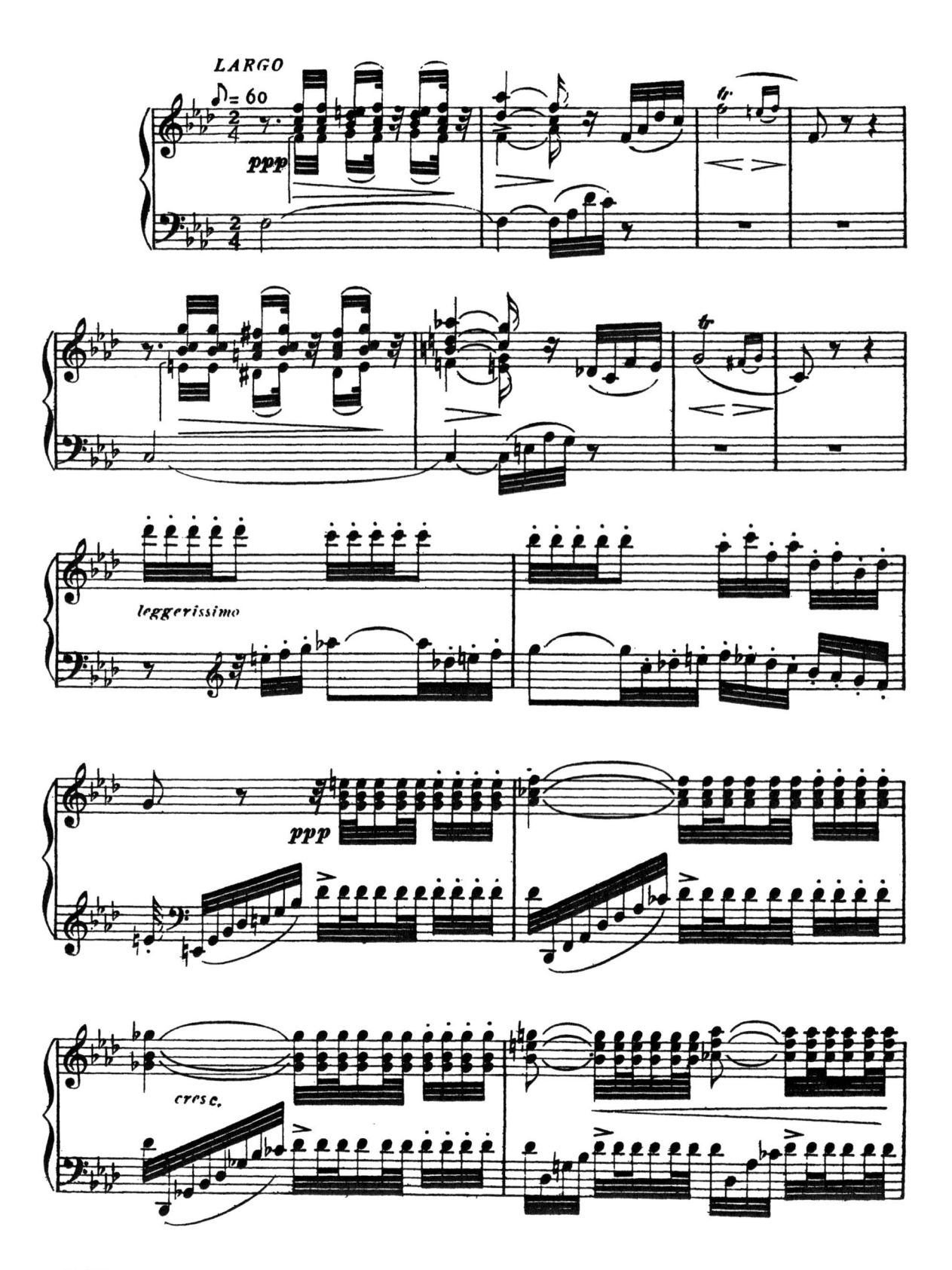

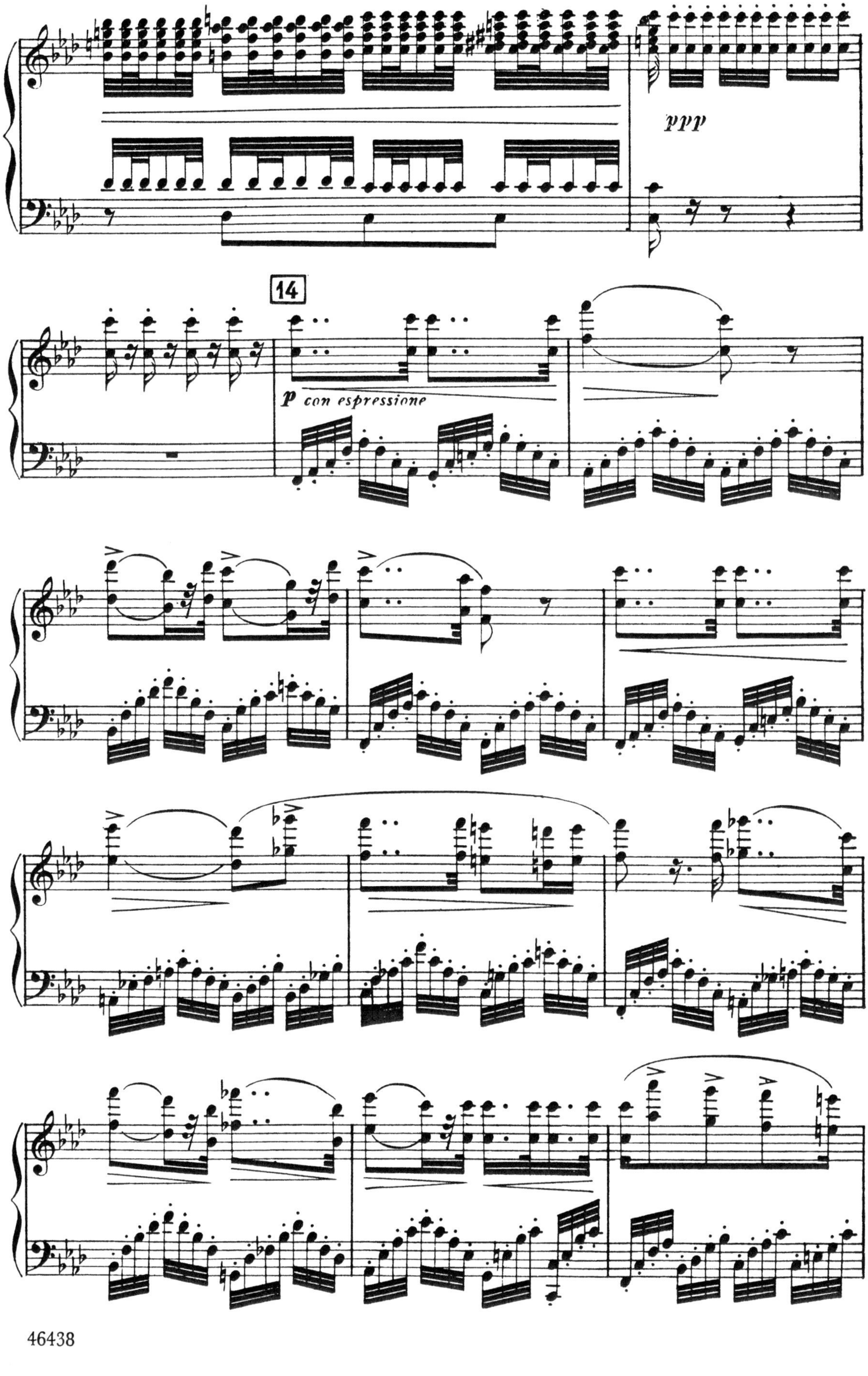
ppp
14
p con espressione

MEDICO Recit.^{vo} molto Adagio   sempre sotto voce

Vegliammo invan due
Two nights we've spent in

281

DAMA: *sempre sotto voce*
In questa apparirà. Ridirlo non debbo ad uom che viva...
To-night she will appear. I dare not repeat it to anyone alive.

MED: Di che parlava nel sonno suo?
Can you remember what she was saying?

(Walking in her sleep, Lady Macbeth enters slowly, carrying a light.)

DAMA: Eccola!
Here she is!

MED: Un lume recasi in man?
How does she come by that lamp?

DAMA: La lampada che sempre si tiene accanto al letto.
She always keeps it lit near her bedside to banish the darkness.

46438

(Lady Macbeth sets the light down and starts rubbing her hands as if to wash them of something.)

Eppur non vede.
Yet she sees noth-ing.

Oh, co - me gli oc - chi spa - lanca!
Behold! Her eyes are wide o - pen!

Lavarsi cre - de.
...as if to wash them.

Perchè sfrega la man?
She is rub-bing her hands

lento dim.

lunga pausa

LADY — AND.te ASSAI SOSTENUTO ♩ = 50 — *sempre sotto voce*

U - na macchia.
Still a spot!

è qui tut - to - ra!
I knew, I knew it!

via, ti
Out, I

283

L
go - - gna! Orsù, t'af_fret_ta! Chi po_
trem - bling. Go on, no mat - ter! Who could
L
te - va in quel ve_gliar - - do tanto sangue immagi_
fan - cy that one so old Would spill so rich a crim-son
stent.
col canto
L
nar, immaginar? chi po - teva tanto sangue immaginar, imma_gi_
flood, So rich and free a crimson flood? How could a man so weak and old spill such a
f
L
nar? Di Fif - fe il
flood?! He, once a
MED.
Che par - lò?
What is she say- ing?
17
f
ppp

285

con dolore
L
prò, no, mai puli - re io non sa-prò?
DAMA
stain, Wipe off my hand this e-vil stain?
f
Oh terror!
Gracious Lord!
MED.
f
Oh terror!
Gracious Lord!
ppp
ff
p
LADY
ppp
Di san-gue u-ma - no sa qui
The smell of blood still is
18
con forza
pp cupo
L
sem-pre. A-rabia in-te - ra rimondar sì piccol
on them. No balm or fra - grance. nor the perfumes of Ar-
L
ma - no co' suoi bal - sa-mi, co' suoi balsami non
a - bia Can turn this hand of mine Sweet-ly-scent-ed once a-

L
dim.
sotto voce
stent.
morendo
può, co' suoi bal - - - sa-mi non può, no, no, non
gain, no fra-grant balm Can ren-der sweet my hand a-
f
p
ppp quasi insensibile
col canto
L
può. Ohi - mè! I panni indossa del - la
MED. gain. A - las! A-way! Be gone! Put on your
Geme?
She's sigh-ing.
ppp
L
notte! Or via, ti sbrat - ta! Banco è spen - - - to, e dalla
night-gown! Be quick, I warn you. Ban-quo's dead, is gone and
L
fos - - - sa chi mo - rì non surse an-
bur - - - ied, And the dead re-turn no

288

LADY
cu - si il tu - o pal - lor. Batte alcuno! Andiam, Mac -
DAMA
pale as nev - er be - fore? Some-one's knock-ing. Let us not
pp cres.
Oh terror! Oh terror!
Gra-cious Lord! Gra-cious Lord!
MED.
pp cres.
Oh terror! Oh terror!
Gra-cious Lord! Gra-cious Lord!
L
betto, andiam, Macbet - - to, no, non t'ac -
wor-ry! Mac-beth, go on! You nev-er
stent.
D
Oh terror!
Gra-cious Lord!
M
Oh terror!
Gra-cious Lord!
20
col canto
L
cu - si il tuo pal - lor, andiam, Macbet - - -
were so pale be - fore. Mac-beth, ah, hur - - -
D
Ah, di lei pie - tà!
Save her, gra - cious Lord!
M
Ah, di lei pie - tà!
Save her, gra - cious Lord!
ppp

ppp e lento
L
to, andiam, andiam, andiam,...andiam, Macbetto, andia -
ry! Mac-beth, be gone! Be gone, Mac-beth, and hur-ry! Be gone, Mac
D
di lei pie - tà!
Al - might - y Lord!
M
di lei pie - tà!
Al - might - y Lord!
(about to leave)
un fil di voce
L
mo, an - - - - - - diam.
beth! Ah!
D
di lei pie - tà, pie - tà!
Save her, al - might - y Lord!
M
di lei pie - tà, pie - tà!
Save her, al - might - y Lord!
pp
pp legg.
ppp morendo

Scene 3

Another Hall in the Castle.

MACB.
Recit.vo
Per-fidi! All' Anglo contro me v'u-nite! Le po-tenze presaghe han profe-
Trai-tors all! A-gainst me on the side of England! Yet I trust in the witch-es proud pre-
Recit.vo
ADAGIO
M
ta-to: „Es-ser puoi sanguina-rio, fe-ro-ce; nes-sun na-to di don-na ti
dic-tion: 'Nei-ther blood-shed nor doubt shall a-larm you. No one born of a wom-an can
ADAGIO
fp
ALLEGRO
nuo-ce!
harm you.'
No, non te-mo di vo-i, nè del fan-
No, your wrath can-not scare me, Nor can the
22
ff ALLEGRO
p
ciullo che vi con-duce! Raffermar sul tro-no quest'as-
ten-der youth who com-mands you. This as-sault will help me, it will
ff

sal-to mi debbe, o sbalzarmi per sempre! Eppur la
height-en my pow-er Or de-stroy me for-ev-er. Yet, deep with-

vi-ta sen-to nelle mie fi-bre i-na-ri-di-ta!
in me the flow of life is dwin-dling and slow-ly freez-ing.

Pie-tà, ri-spet-to, a-mo-re, con-
The love, re-spect, de-vo-tion, an

for-to a'dì ca-den-ti, ah! non spargeran d'un
old man's prize en-chant-ed, To me will not be

fio — re la tu_a_canu_ta e _ tà, non spargeran, non sparge-
grant — ed. For me no__tear will fall, And on my tomb nev-er will

ran d'un fio_re la tu_a ca_nu_ta____ e _ tà.
bloom The ros-es of mem'ry on which a tear____ may fall.

Nè sul tuo re _ gio__ sas _ so spe_rar so_a_vi ac-
Nor will the soft sounds of cry _ ing Be heard when Mac-beth will be

centi; ah! sol la bestem_mia, ahi las _ so! la ne_nia tua sa-
dy-ing. No! On _ ly the mum-bling of curs _ es will be my fi _ nal

cresc.
con forza
dim.
M
rà, la nenia tua sa - rà, sol la bestemmia, sol la be_stem - mia, ahi
call. Yes, I can hear them all, fear-ful and ly - ing, Ev - er de - ny the se - cret
24
p
las - so! la ne_nia tua sa_rà, ahi
curs - es that sound my fi - nal call. Yes,
dolciss.
las - - so! la ne - nia tu - a sa_rà,
curs - - es de - nied but ut - tered by all!
con forza
ah! sol la bestem - mia, - ahi
Ah! On - ly a thun - der - of

las - so! la_ nenia tu a sa-
curs - es will_ be my_ fi - nal

rà, ahi las - - - -
call, Of curs - - - -

so! sol_ la bestemmia, ahi lasso! la ne_ nia, la nenia tua sa
es! On - ly the sound of curs-es and sigh - - ing Will be my fi-nal

rà.
call.

297

298

MACB.
Che fu? quali nuove?
What news? Our lot's improving!
Sire! La fo-
Sire! The
Sire! La fo-
Sire! The
(thunderstruck)
M
M'hai deluso, infernale pre-
Ah, the prophets from Hell did de-
resta di Birnam si muove!
Forest of Birnam is moving!
resta di Birnam si muove!
Forest of Birnam is moving!
M
sagio! Qui l'usbergo, la spada, il pu-
ceive me. Bring my harness, my helmet, and my

300

BATTAGLIA

ALL.ᵗᵗᵒ VIVO ♩ = 120

ria! / ry!

ria! / ry!

ria! / ry!

28 *ALL.ᵗᵗᵒ VIVO* ♩ = 120

Interno *fff*

(The scene shifts to a vast plain bordered by hills and forests. To the rear, a line of English soldiers is seen advancing under a cover of branches carried by each man.)

46438

MACDUFF: Via le fronde, e mano all'armi!
Drop the branches and grab your weapons!

mi seguite!
On to battle!

(Malcolm, Macduff, and the soldiers off.)

CORO di SOLDATI
Tenori: All'armi! all'armi!
To battle! to battle!

Bassi: All'armi! all'armi!
To battle! to battle!

303

304

(Enters Macbeth pursued by Macduff.)

MACDUFF
Car- ne - - - fi - ce de' fi - gli miei, t'ho giunto.
Ah, mur - - - d'rer of the ones I loved, I'll kill you!

MACBETH
Fuggi! nato di donna uccidermi non può. Nato non sono: strappato fui dal sen materno.
No one born of a woman can ever strike me dead. I was not born, but ripped untimely from the womb.

46438

305

(frantic with terror)
MACB. (They both brandish their swords and exit battling.)

Cie - lo!
Sa - tan!

34
(Enter a group of Scottish women and children.)

CORO di DONNE
Sop. 1ⁱ. e 2ⁱ.
ff In - - fau - sto gior - - no!
Death and dis - as - - ter!

Sop. 3ⁱ. e 4ⁱ.
ff In - - fau - sto gior - - no!
Death and dis - as - - ter!

46438

306

Pre-ghiam pe' fi-gli no-stri!
May God pro-tect our chil-dren!

Pre-ghiam pe' fi-gli no-stri!
May God pro-tect our chil-dren!

CORO di DONNE

Ces-sa il fra-gor!
Mer-cy, o Lord!

ancor più piano

morendo

dim. ed allarg.

46438

Finale

CORO DI DONNE / CORO INTERNO

Vit-to-ria! / Oh glo-ry!
Vit-to-ria! / Oh glo-ry!
Vit-to-ria! / Oh glo-ry!
Vit-to-ria! / Oh glo-ry!

(Enter Malcolm and English soldiers dragging in Macbeth's men as prisoners. Macduff, other soldiers, bards, and people start filling the stage.)

MALCOLM
O-ve s'è fit-to l'usurpa-tor?
Where is the ty-rant? Where does he hide?

MACD.
Co-là da me tra-
He's ly-ing where I

(on bended knee)
Mf.
fit - to.
killed him.
Sal - ve, o
God save the
37
Re!
King,
Sal - ve, o Re!
save the King!
CORO
Sop.
Sal - ve, o Re!
God save the King!
Ten.
Sal - ve, o Re!
God save the King!
Bassi.
Sal - ve, o Re!
God save the King!

309

310

311

SOLDATI: glì è, ____ l'e ro e e gli è che spense il tra di tor. La
lead ____ us on to glo ry on the field of war. We

pa __ tria, il Re sal vò; ____ a lui o nor, o nor e glo ri
hon ___ or him who freed ____ our hap less broth ers from the yoke they

BARDI: Mac beth, ____ Macbeth ov' è? do
Mac beth, ____ Mac beth is dead. The

SOLDATI: a!
bore.

BARDI
v'è l'usur - pa - tor? D'un sof - fio il ful - mi -
ty - - rant is no more, De - stroyed by wrath and
v'è l'usur - pa - tor? D'un sof - fio il ful - mi -
ty - - rant is no more, De - stroyed by wrath and
DONNE
Sop. 1i e 2i
40 legato e dolce
p
Sal - gan mie
Fa - ther in
Sop. 3i
Sal - gan mie
Fa - ther in
BARDI
nò, il ful - minò, d'un soffio il Dio della vitto - ria.
fu - ry of the Lord, Our God al - might - y and vic-to - rious!
nò, il ful - minò, d'un soffio il Dio della vitto - ria.
fu - ry of the Lord, Our God al - might - y and vic-to - rious!
dolciss.
ppp

313

DONNE

grazie a te, gran Dio vendi_ca_tor; a chi ne li_be_rò in_ni can_
Heav'n a-bove, our thanks we sing to Thee, While pledg-ing all our faith and love to

MACD.

S'af_fi_ _ _di o gnun_ _ _ _al
O King, _ _ _ be-nign and just, _ _ _ with law and

MALC.

Con fi_ _ _da, o Sco_ _ _zia, in
A King _ _ _ has turned to dust, _ _ _ a reign of

tiam di glo_ _ria.
him who made us free.

tiam di glo_ _ria.
him who made us free.

46438

314

ff
B
pro - de eroe e_gliè che spen - se il tra_di _tor! La
he - ro's heart has led us on to win the war: We
S
41
pa - tria, il Re sal_vò; a lui onor, o_nor e gloria, onor e glo - -
hon - - or him who saved our no-ble King And freed our country, proud and glo - -

316

317

Re, s'af-fi-di al Re,
God, al-might-y God!

me, t'af-fi-da in me,
God, al-might-y God!

te, mie gra-zie a te,
Lord, al-might-y God!

te, mie gra-zie a te,
Lord, al-might-y God!

glo-ria, il pro- - de eroe egli è che spense il tra-di-
coun-try! A he- -ro's heart has led us on to win the

glo-ria, il pro- - de eroe egli è che spense il tra-di-
coun-try! A he- -ro's heart has led us on to win the

glo-ria, il pro- - de eroe egli è che spense il tra-di-
coun-try! A he- -ro's heart has led us on to win the

glo-ria, il pro- - de eroe egli è che spense il tra-di-
coun-try! A he- -ro's heart has led us on to win the

319

320

End of the Opera.